The Baseball Trivia and Facts Book for Kids

A History of Major League Baseball with Biographies, Rules and Playing Tips for Young Readers

Ty McDaniel

Disclaimer

Without the publisher's prior written consent, no portion of this publication may be reproduced, stored in a retrieval system, or transmitted in any form or by any means, electronic, mechanical, photocopying, recording, scanning, or otherwise, except as permitted under Sections 107 or 108 of the United States Copyright Act of 1976. Although every precaution has been taken in preparing this book, the publisher is not liable for any mistakes, omissions, or damages resulting from the use of the material included within. This book is intended solely for entertainment and educational purposes. The opinions presented are those of the author alone and should not be construed as professional advice or directives. The reader's activities are his or her own responsibility. The author and publisher take no responsibility or liability for the purchaser or reader of these contents. The reader is responsible for his or her own usage of any products or techniques referenced in this publication.

The Baseball Trivia and Facts Book for Kids
First Edition: August 15, 2023
Copyright © 2023 Caliber Brands Inc.

Contents

Introduction	5
1. The Origins of Baseball: How the Game Came to Life	7
2. The Basic Rules of Baseball: How the Game is Played	13
3. Baseball Positions: Exploring How Teams Work	25
4. Famous Ballparks: Exploring the Places Where Games Happen	50
5. Baseball Heroes: Legendary Players of the Game	63
6. The Greatest Teams That Ruled the Field	74
7. Little League Starter Guide for Beginners	102
8. Baseball Trivia for Young Fans	124
Conclusion	141

Introduction

Welcome to the fascinating history of baseball, which is packed with captivating tales of the sport's greatest players and epic games that have contributed to its rich past and enduring legacy. For more than a century, baseball has been able to captivate the hearts and minds of millions from its humble beginnings to becoming the most popular pastime in the United States. This book not only dives into the rich history and famous moments of Major League Baseball, but will also help you step onto the diamond for the first time with useful tips and strategies.

In the following chapters, we will explore the origins of baseball, tracing its evolution from basic village games to a national obsession. We will revisit the legendary moments of teams such as the Boston Red Sox, New York Yankees, and

Los Angeles Dodgers, as well as meet the legendary players who have left their mark on the field.

However, this book is not merely a history lesson-- prepare to jump straight onto the diamond! You will learn the unique skills and strategies required for each position, from the pitcher on the mound to the shortstop defending the infield. Learn how to pitch, catch, bat, and run like a pro, as well as the importance of teamwork needed for every exciting play.

Now grab your cap and lace up your cleats, and get ready to learn all about what goes into making baseball such an important part of American culture. Batter up!

Chapter 1
The Origins of Baseball: How the Game Came to Life

American baseball can be traced back to bat-and-ball games that originated in ancient Egypt, Greece, and Rome. Each culture's version of the game involving hitting a ball with a stick or hand and each had its own set of rules.

As time progressed, these bat and ball games developed in Medieval England and Europe into games known as "stoolball" and "rounders." Rounders was played with a ball and a bat, whereas stoolball featured hitting the ball with a flat paddle. Both games included base running and gradually included rules that were refined in modern American baseball.

Baseball as we know it now originated in North America in the 18th and 19th centuries. The game became popular in rural areas, where it was played on homemade grounds governed by changing rules. Baseball's early iterations were frequently disorganized and lacked consistent rules.

In the early nineteenth century, a game known as "town ball" was popular in New England. Town ball was a bat-and-ball game similar to baseball, although the regulations varied based on the locality. The game required hitting a ball and running bases, although the exact rules varied depending on where it was played.

The Knickerbocker Rules

In 1845, a man named Alexander Cartwright organized a group of young men in New York City to form the Knickerbocker Base Ball Club. Cartwright is widely credited with formalizing many of the rules that have become essential to contemporary baseball. The Knickerbocker Rules defined a diamond-shaped field, the number of players for each team, and the concept of three strikes for an out and three outs per inning.

The Knickerbocker Rules helped standardize the game and laid the framework for baseball's popularity to spread. Baseball clubs and leagues began to establish in various sections of the United States, and the sport gained popularity in both urban and rural areas. Baseball rapidly grew during the Civil War, when soldiers from several regions brought their versions of the game to military barracks, resulting in exchanges and the merging of numerous rules.

The first official baseball game played under the Knickerbocker Rules took place on June 19, 1846, at Elysian Fields in Hoboken, New Jersey. The famous Knickerbocker Base Ball Club, led by Alexander Cartwright, hosted the game against the New York Nine, another baseball team. The game was played at a slower tempo than modern baseball, with pitchers delivering the ball at a slower pace compared to today's pitchers. The batter's objective was to make contact and put the ball in play.

The game itself became hotly contested. The Knickerbocker Club's members were well-versed in the Knickerbocker Rules, having played countless practice games before the historic match— However, the New York Nine were used to playing a different brand of baseball and had to change their strategy to comply with the new rules. Ultimately, the Knickerbocker Rules placed a large emphasis on teamwork and strategy, allowing the players to learn how to employ these components to their advantage. The Knickerbocker Club defeated the New York Nine in a hard-fought game.

The Birth of the National & American Leagues

The National League began in 1876 as baseball's first professional league. The organization provided professional baseball with structure when it was founded with just eight teams. In addition to establishing baseball as a professional sport, the creation of the league led to the establishment of official statistics and records.

As baseball's popularity expanded, it encountered challenges. The National League's control over player salary led to widespread dissatisfaction among players and team owners. Thus, the National League formed the American League in 1901 and competition for players and fans intensified.

In 1903, nine teams came together to form what would become Major League Baseball (MLB). The National League and American League owners agreed to hold a peace conference to work out their differences and create a more solid and well-organized structure for professional baseball. Chicago's Leland Hotel served as the site for the meeting in January of 1903.

In order to better manage and coordinate their operations, the two leagues decided at the peace conference to form a unified entity called as Major League Baseball. The first World Series was established in the same year by pitting the National League champion against the American League champion in a best-of-nine playoff series.

Later that same year, in October 1903, the Pittsburgh Pirates of the National League faced the Boston Americans (now the Boston Red Sox) of the American League in the first official World Series. The Boston Americans won the World Series in a best-of-nine series, winning five games to three and becoming the first club to do it.

The success of the first World Series helped to cement the alliance between the National League and the American League, paving the way for future cooperation and collaboration between the two leagues. MLB has grown and evolved throughout the years, introducing new teams, expanding its reach, and becoming a vital part of American sports culture.

Dead Ball Era

There are two major eras in baseball history that have had a considerable impact on the game's style and dynamics: the Dead Ball Era and the Live Ball Era. The Dead Ball Era, which lasted from the early 1900s through the late 1910s, was distinguished by low-scoring games and a focus on pitching and limited ball strategies. Baseballs were less active during this time period, resulting in restricted power hitting and an emphasis on strategic tactics like bunting and base stealing. However, the game underwent a dramatic shift around 1920, with the introduction of a new, more active ball and regulations that benefited hitters. This marked the start of the Live Ball Era, which resulted in improved offensive play, more home runs, and higher-scoring games. The contrast between these two eras demonstrates how changes in equipment and rules impacted the growth of America's favorite pastime.

Further League Changes

Baseball, like most of American society, was segregated for a long time. African American players had their own leagues where great athletes could show off their abilities. However, Jackie Robinson broke the color barrier by signing with the

Brooklyn Dodgers in 1947, becoming the first African American to play in Major League Baseball. Robinson's participation paved the path for more African-American players to join the big leagues, forever altering the face of the sport.

Major League Baseball grew and evolved in the latter half of the twentieth century. The addition of new teams and expansion into new cities, as well as advances in technology and media coverage, have all contributed to the sport's growing popularity. Baseball became a national pastime thanks to television, which brought it into households across the country.

Major League Baseball now has 30 teams, 15 in each of the National and American Leagues. The creation of MLB in 1903 was a pivotal moment in baseball history, laying the groundwork for nearly a century of thrilling baseball that continues to thrive today.

Chapter 2
The Basic Rules of Baseball: How the Game is Played

Get ready, young baseball fan, to learn everything there is to know about this amazing sport. In this chapter, we'll cover the fundamental rules that make baseball so entertaining to both play and watch. The fundamental goal of baseball is for a team to score more runs than their opponent by batting, running the bases, and guarding the field. The offense's goal is for its batters to hit the ball without being caught by the defensive team and proceed around the bases, eventually crossing home plate and scoring runs. Meanwhile, the defensive team seeks to keep opposing batters from scoring by fielding the ball, throwing strikeout pitches, and catching outfield balls.

Runs

Runs are the primary unit of scoring in baseball, and they are gained when a player from the offensive team successfully completes a lap around all three bases and crosses home plate without being tagged out.

A home run is one of the most thrilling methods to score runs. It is awarded when a batter connects with the ball and sends it out into the playing field, usually over the outfield fence. The hitter, along with any other runners on base at the time, is permitted to jog around the bases and score a run each.

Runs can be scored in a variety of ways other than home runs. A batter can get a hit by successfully hitting the ball into the field of play and safely reaching any base while the defense attempts to retrieve the ball and throw it back to the infield. A run is scored if the batter can round all three bases and cross home plate before being tagged out by the defense.

The offensive team can also score runs through base on balls, often known as walks. If a pitcher throws four balls outside the strike zone, the batter is awarded first base. If the bases are loaded at the time, the player on third base advances and scores a run.

Players

At any given time, the defensive team has nine active players on the ballfield. They include the catcher, pitcher, first baseman, second baseman, third baseman, shortstop, left fielder, center fielder and right fielder.

Innings

A typical baseball game is divided into nine innings. Each inning is divided into two halves, with one side batting and the other team fielding.

Fair and Foul Territory

The baseball field is split into fair and foul area. A fair ball is one that is hit between the baselines and landed in fair territory. If the ball lands outside the baselines, it is a foul ball.

The rules governing foul and fair balls in baseball are critical to the game's dynamics and the outcome of each at-bat. A fair ball is one that is batted and landed within the field of play, which is defined by the foul lines that run from home plate to the outfield boundaries. It can touch or cross over any of the bases, allowing the batter to become a base runner. A foul ball, on the other hand, is a batted ball that lands outside or goes beyond the foul lines before reaching first or third base. When a foul ball is hit, play is halted and the pitch is not counted as a strike or a ball. The batter continues to bat until they hit a fair ball, strike out, or reach base safely. A foul tip is a sort of foul ball that occurs when the batter makes slight contact with the pitch and directs it towards the catcher's mitt or hand. A foul tip, unlike a standard foul ball, is considered a live ball and counts as a strike.

Understanding these distinctions is critical for assessing a batter's progress and the state of play during a baseball game.

Batting

The offensive team takes turns batting. The batter stands at home plate, while the pitcher from the opposite team throws the ball to the catcher. The batter's goal is to hit the ball into fair territory.

If the batter misses the ball and it hits the strikeout zone, the batter is out.

Outs

The batting team continues to bat until three outs happen. An out is recorded when the following occurs:

- The batter strikes out (receives three strikes).
- A flyout occurs when a batter hits a fair ball but the defense catches it before it hits the ground.
- A fielder with the ball tags a runner who is not on a base.
- A fielder throws the ball to a base, and the base is tagged, before the runner arrives.

Pitch Count & Balls

The pitch count is the number of pitches thrown by a pitcher during a game or inning. It is an important statistic for managing a pitcher's workload and preventing overuse, lowering the chance of injury. To protect players' arms, different leagues and age groups may impose certain pitch count limits. Coaches regularly monitor pitch counts and frequently opt to pull a pitcher from the game when they reach a certain limit.

Balls, on the other hand, are pitches that are thrown outside the strike zone but are not struck by the hitter. When a pitcher pitches four balls to a hitter, the batter is given first base, which is referred to as a "walk."

The strike zone is an imaginary area above home plate that decides whether a pitch is a strike or a ball. A strike is defined as any pitch that crosses the strike zone but is not swung at by the hitter. The count, which is stated as "balls" followed by "strikes," represents the batter's current number of balls and strikes. During an at-bat, the count is critical in determining whether the pitcher has an advantage or whether the batter has an advantage. A full count of "3-2" indicates three balls and two strikes, indicating a vital moment in the game.

Baserunning & Stealing

Base running in baseball refers to the act of running from one base to another while adhering to certain rules. There are four bases on the field: first base, second base, third base, and home plate. They are placed in a diamond pattern.

Players must stay within the lines and not venture outside the diamond. They can advance to the next base when the ball is hit, caught, or walked. If they catch a ball in the air, they must return to their starting base before running again. When a new player needs a base, the others must advance. They are unable to pass each other.

Base stealing occurs when a baserunner attempts to move to the next base while the pitcher retains the ball. Before attempting to steal, the runner must take a leadoff. They are not permitted to steal while the pitcher is pitching. Following the appropriate order, only one base can be stolen at a time. Baserunners must tag up on caught fly balls, and defensive interference is not permitted. Balks by the pitcher might result in an extra base for the runner. Successful steals result in a stolen base in the runner's statistics. Base stealing requires speed, timing, and awareness, but it is also dangerous if the runner is caught since they can be struck out.

Strike Zone

The strike zone is an important part of baseball, and it is determined by precise standards listed in the official rules. It is an imaginary space over home plate that extends to both sides of the plate's midline and has a width equal to home plate's 17-inch width. The strike zone is commonly defined as the distance between the top of the batter's shoulders and waist and the top of their knees. However, there is some subjectivity involved in calling balls and strikes, and umpires may interpret the strike zone differently. Umpires are encouraged to remain consistent in their strike zone calls throughout the game in order to ensure fairness and consistency. The batter's stance in the batter's box can influence the umpire's assessment of the strike zone, although umpires should not penalize batters for stooping or standing tall.

Substitutions

During the game, teams can make changes, substituting players for various strategic or defensive purposes.

Extra Innings

If the game is still tied after nine innings, extra innings are played until one team wins after a complete inning.

Inning Changes

After each team's offensive half of the inning is complete, the teams trade positions on the field. The offensive team becomes the defensive team in the bottom half of the inning, and vice versa.

If a game is suspended or tied due to weather or other causes in professional baseball or some high-level amateur leagues, it may be resumed at a later date and continue from where it left off. This scenario could result in games lasting longer than the standard nine innings.

Umpires

Umpires play crucial roles in baseball, overseeing the game and guaranteeing its fair and abides by the rules. During a professional game, there are usually four umpires on the field, each with their own set of responsibilities. The home plate umpire is responsible for calling balls and strikes, as well as evaluating whether pitches lie within the strike zone. They also make decisions on hit-by-pitches, walks, and home-plate interference. Meanwhile, the three base umpires are stationed at first, second, and third base, respectively. They are in charge of calling plays at their respective bases, including as determining whether runners are safe or out and handling tag-ups and force-outs. Umpires work together as a team to make correct judgments on close or complex plays. They have the authority to expel players, coaches, or managers who break the rules or act unsportsmanlike. Furthermore, several baseball leagues use video review systems to allow umpires to confirm certain calls, assuring fairness and precision in officiating. Umpires are supposed to be impartial and professional during the game, upholding the regulations and protecting the sport's integrity. Their knowledge and judgment are critical in preserving a level playing field and ensuring a pleasant and impartial baseball game.

Terminology

Here are some commonly used terms that will help you better follow the game along with the rules just discussed.

- **At-bats:** The number of times a batter steps up to bat and faces a pitcher.
- **Base hit**: A clean hit that allows the batter to reach base safely.

- **Batting average (BA):** The percentage of a player's at-bats that result in base hits.
- **Clutch hitter:** A player who performs exceptionally well in high-pressure or critical game situations.
- **Double:** A hit that allows the batter to reach second base safely.
- **Earned run average (ERA):** A pitcher's average number of earned runs allowed per nine innings pitched.
- **Error:** A fielding mistake that allows a batter or baserunner to reach base or advance.
- **Fly ball:** A batted ball hit into the air in the outfield.
- **Groundball:** A batted ball that rolls along the ground.
- **Left on base (LOB):** The number of baserunners who are stranded on the bases at the end of an inning.
- **On-base percentage (OBP):** The percentage of times a player reaches base safely, including hits, walks, and hit by pitch.
- **Pitcher's duel:** A low-scoring game in which both starting pitchers perform exceptionally well.
- **Quality start:** A pitching performance in which a starting pitcher allows three earned runs or fewer in six or more innings pitched.
- **RBI (Runs Batted In):** A statistic credited to a batter who successfully allows a teammate to score a run.

- **Sacrifice bunt:** A strategic bunt by the batter to advance a baserunner at the expense of the batter's chance to reach base.
- **Triple:** A hit that allows the batter to reach third base safely.

Recent Changes to Major League Rules

Several recent adjustments to Major League Baseball regulations have been established to address various aspects of the game, including pace of play, player safety, and competition. Knowing about recent revisions to MLB regulations is critical because it keeps us up to date on how the game is currently played.

Pitcher Substance Checks

MLB increased pitcher checks during games in order to enforce laws involving foreign substances on baseballs. Umpires were empowered to scrutinize pitchers' caps, gloves, belts, and other equipment for any foreign substances that could potentially impact the baseball's grip and movement.

Three-Batter Minimum for Pitchers

Starting with the 2020 season, pitchers must face at least three batters or pitch until the end of the half-inning before being relieved, unless injured. This rule was put in place to limit the number of pitching changes and to speed up the game.

Runner on Second in Extra Innings

To shorten extra-inning games, MLB instituted a regulation for the pandemic-shortened 2020 season that put a runner on second base at the start of each half-inning in extra innings. This rule was designed to maximize the likelihood of scoring and speed up the completion of games.

Expanded Playoffs

MLB increased the playoff field from 10 to 16 teams for the 2020 season, with the top two teams from each division making the postseason. This modification allowed more teams to compete in the playoffs, increasing the postseason's excitement and competition.

Seven-Inning Doubleheaders

As part of the pandemic-related modifications, MLB instituted seven-inning games for planned doubleheaders during the 2020 and 2021 seasons. This adjustment sought to reduce player fatigue and the amount of games played in a compressed schedule.

Position Player Pitching

To avoid misuse of pitchers in some games, MLB authorized teams to deploy position players as pitchers in certain scenarios during the 2020 and 2021 seasons.

Electronic Strike Zone (Testing in the Minor Leagues)

MLB has been testing the use of an automated electronic strike zone in select Minor League Baseball games to evaluate its accuracy and potential future use in the major leagues.

It's important to remember that MLB may continue to experiment with and implement rule changes to improve the game's competitiveness, safety, and fan experience. Rules and policies are subject to review and adjustment depending on feedback from players, clubs, and fans, as well as the league's efforts to stay current with the developing landscape of professional baseball.

In this chapter, you have learned all about the rules of baseball and recent changes the major league has implemented. With this deeper understanding, you will now be able to follow the game with greater attention to the action at play.

Chapter 3
Baseball Positions: Exploring How Teams Work

As we've previously discussed, the origins of the baseball positions can be traced back to the mid-19th century. As baseball evolved from its predecessors like rounders, stool ball and town ball, players and teams began to adopt more specialized defensive positions to improve their strategy and efficiency.

The positions in baseball were primarily influenced by the need to cover different areas of the field effectively and respond to different types of hits and offensive plays. Without further ado, let's take a deeper look into each of these positions and how they work together to build a powerful team.

Pitcher

The pitcher is one of baseball's most significant and specialized roles. They are vital to the game because they establish the tempo, regulate the strike zone, and prevent the opposing side from scoring runs.

The pitcher's primary goal after tossing a ball to the hitter is to strike them out. The pitcher and catcher work together to choose the optimal pitch to throw based on each batter's strengths and weaknesses. They must be able to judge the situation and adjust their pitch accordingly. Pitchers also need to keep an eye on runners on base to prevent bases from being stolen and runners advancing.

Pitch Types

- **Fastball:** The fastball is a high-speed pitch that is thrown with maximum velocity and minimal movement. It is often used to challenge hitters and establish control of the strike zone.
- **Breaking Balls:** Breaking balls, such as curveballs and sliders, have significant side movement, making them challenging for batters to hit. These pitches are used to deceive hitters and induce swings and misses.
- **Changeup:** The changeup is a slower pitch designed to look like a fastball but with reduced speed. It is used to disrupt a hitter's timing and cause weak contact with the bat.

Pitching Rules

- **Balks:** Pitchers are not allowed to deceive baserunners by making illegal movements while on the mound. A balk is called if the pitcher makes a deceptive move or fails to come to a complete stop in their delivery.
- **Pitching Distance:** The pitcher's rubber, located 60 feet 6 inches from home plate, marks the pitching distance. Pitchers must release the ball from behind the rubber when throwing to the batter.
- **Intentional Walks:** Managers may choose to intentionally walk a batter by signaling to the umpire rather than having the pitcher throw four pitches outside the strike zone.

Pitch Count and Fatigue

As mentioned in the previous chapter, pitchers have a limited pitch count to prevent overuse and reduce the risk of injury. The pitch count varies based on factors such as age, level of play, and pitch type. Managers and coaches must monitor a pitcher's workload and determine when to replace them if they are fatigued or nearing their pitch limit.

Catcher

The catcher position in baseball is both demanding and important on the field. Catchers are known as "field generals" because they are in charge of coordinating the defense, managing the pitching staff, and contributing significantly to the overall strategy of the game. Their major role is to receive pitcher pitches and cleanly catch the ball, while also framing pitches to present them as strikes, providing their pitchers an edge in the strike zone. Catchers collaborate closely with pitchers, learning their strengths and limitations and calling the appropriate pitches to exploit the batter's shortcomings. They also play an important part in coordinating infield and outfield defensive positioning, talking with other players to guide their placements based on the batter.

Catchers must also be skilled at blocking balls in the dirt to prevent baserunners from advancing and making accurate throws to bases to capture potential stealing runners. They are responsible for a variety of defensive plays, including catching pop-ups in foul territory and making defensive catches at home plate on bunts or close plays.

To protect oneself from potential injuries caused by foul balls, wild pitches, and collisions at home plate, catchers wear specialized protective gear. These include a chest protector, leg guards, a helmet, and a mask.

Responsibilities

- **Managing the Pitching Staff:** Catchers collaborate extensively with pitchers, learning their strengths, weaknesses, and preferred pitch sequences. They must call the correct pitches in order to exploit the batter's flaws and set up strikeouts or weak hits.
- **Defensive Plays:** Catchers play an important role in coordinating the defensive placement of the infield and outfield. They communicate with other players, directing where they should place themselves in relation to the batter and the game circumstances. Catchers must be good at stopping balls in the dirt in order to prevent runners from advancing and keep control of the game. They must also be able to make accurate throws to the bases in order to catch baserunners attempting to steal.
- **Framing Pitches:** Catchers employ subtle gestures to frame pitches, giving the umpire the impression that they are strikes. By delivering the ball well, a skilled catcher can influence the umpire's decision.
- **Wild Pitches and Passed Balls:** A passed ball occurs when a catcher fails to handle a catchable pitch, allowing a baserunner to advance. A wild pitch happens when a pitcher throws a pitch that the catcher cannot manage, allowing baserunners to advance. Both occurrences assist the opposition team in getting closer to a run.

- **Throw Downs:** Catchers must be skilled at making quick and accurate throws to bases in order to catch baserunners attempting to steal. In these plays, timing and precision are critical.

Catchers are prohibited from interfering with the batter's swing or obstructing a baserunner's route. Interference can result in penalties or baserunner advancement.

Overall, the catcher position requires outstanding defensive skills, leadership, and a thorough knowledge of the game. They act as a vital communicator between the pitchers and the rest of the team. Their ability to successfully handle pitching is key to a team's success. Catchers frequently become the team's heart and soul, displaying the spirit of hard work, resilience, and dedication that makes up baseball.

Infield Positions - First Base, Second Base, Third Base, and Shortstop

Baseball's infield positions arose from the need to cover the bases and field balls hit in the infield. As the game progressed, players were assigned specific tasks such as covering each base and making plays on ground balls and infield hits. The shortstop position, in particular, became an important position to cover the region between second and third base, where many balls were hit during early games.

First Base

In baseball, the first base position is a critical and fundamental defensive position on the field. Fielding ground balls, receiving throws from other infielders, and covering the first base bag during defensive plays are all important roles for first basemen. Their major task is to precisely receive throws and record outs. They must have quick reflexes and good hand-eye coordination to field ground balls and make accurate throws to other bases, or to the pitcher covering first base. First basemen are responsible for keeping baserunners close to the base to prevent stolen bases and disrupt the other team's running game. They must be able to stretch and be flexible in order to catch throws that may not be on target, since this might mean the difference between an out and a safe call. First basemen, like all fielders, must be aware of fair and foul territory in order to field the ball correctly.

To record an out, a first baseman must have one foot on (or touching) the base when receiving throws. They must also avoid interfering with the batter or blocking the baserunner's path to first base, as interference can result in penalties or baserunner advancement. Overall, first basemen are critical to the team's defensive strategy and considerably contribute to the team's overall performance on the field.

In baseball, the first base position is a critical defensive position on the field. First basemen are essential for fielding ground balls, covering the first base bag during defensive plays, and adding to the team's overall success. The following are the most important components of the first base position, including their responsibilities and the rules that regulate their actions:

Fielding Responsibilities

- **Receiving Throws:** The first baseman's primary role during defensive plays is to accept throws from other infielders, particularly the third baseman and pitcher. They must be capable of catching balls thrown to first base and recording outs.
- **Holding Runners:** When baserunners reach first, first basemen are also responsible for keeping them close to the base. They limit the chance of stolen bases by preventing runners from gaining a considerable lead.
- **Covering First Base:** When the ball is hit to other infielders, the first baseman must be in position to cover the base. This requires insight and the ability to read the game at play.
- **Stretching for Throws:** First basemen must be flexible and able to stretch for long throws. Stretching properly can assist runners secure outs and prevent them from reaching base safely.

Regulations and Rules

When receiving throws to first base, the first baseman must have one foot on or near the base. If this is not done, the runner may be judged safe even if the throw is caught.

- **Tagging Runners:** If a throw to first base is delayed, the first baseman may attempt to tag the runner with the ball. Another approach to record an out is to tag the runner before they reach the base.
- **Fair and foul territory:** First basemen, like all fielders, must be aware of fair and foul territory. Fielding a ball in foul territory is termed a foul ball, and runners cannot progress.
- **Interference Rules:** First basemen must avoid interfering with the batter or blocking the baserunner's path to first base. Interference can result in penalties or baserunner advancement.

The first base position necessitates defensive abilities, quick reflexes, and superb hand-eye coordination. First basemen must be capable of catching and fielding balls thrown to them and must collaborate with other infielders to properly perform defensive plays. They also help to control the opposing team's running game by keeping runners near the base. Overall, first basemen are essential to the defense and significantly contribute to the team's overall performance.

Short Stop

Baseball's shortstop position is dynamic and important on the field. Shortstops are very competent defensive players that cover a huge area between second and third base, make difficult plays on ground balls hit in their area, and have high alertness. Turning double plays requires them to field the ball quickly, tag second base (or step on it), and make accurate throws to first base. Shortstops also work with other infielders, acting as "captains of the infield," to ensure appropriate positioning and efficient defensive plays. They must be extremely aware of their surroundings to predict baserunners' movements and react appropriately. Because of their powerful throwing arms, quick reflexes, and fielding skills, they are defensive playmakers who make a huge impact on the team's success by preventing runs and contributing to outs.

Fielding Responsibilities

Shortstops play a key role on defense, as they must be able to cover a broad area between second and third base and participate in both infield and outfield plays. Here are the most important components of playing shortstop:

- **Ranging Plays:** Shortstops are recognized for their great range and quickness, which allows them to field ground balls hit close to them and make difficult plays on balls hit deep in the hole between third base and shortstop.
- **Double Plays:** Shortstops play an important part in turning double plays. To complete the double play, they must immediately field the ball, tag second base (or step on it), and make a quick, accurate throw to first base.

- **Covering Second Base:** When a ground ball is hit to the second baseman, the shortstop must be ready to take the throw.
- **Communication and coordination:** Shortstops frequently function as "captains of the infield," coordinating with fellow infielders to ensure proper positioning and defensive plays. They must have exceptional situational awareness, which includes knowing where baserunners are and anticipating the likely results of various plays.
- **Tagging and Force Outs:** When attempting to make an out on a baserunner, shortstops must apply tags when the runner is not forced to advance and touch (or step on) the base to record force outs when the runner is forced to advance.

Shortstops, like all fielders, must be aware of fair and foul territory and react accordingly to balls hit in those areas. Shortstops must also avoid interfering with the batter or impeding baserunners' routes, as interference can result in penalties or baserunner advancement.

The umpire may use the infield fly rule if a pop-up with sufficient height and a likelihood of being caught by an infielder is hit. In a situation with runners on base, this rule instantly strikes the hitter out to prevent a double or triple play.

Second Base

In baseball, the second base position plays an important and flexible function on the field. Second basemen are critical defensive players that cover the area between first and second base and turn double plays. Their main role during defensive plays is to cover second base, positioning oneself to receive throws from other infielders and tag the base to record force outs. Second basemen are crucial in turning double plays alongside the shortstop, receiving the ball and delivering quick, accurate throws to finish the play. They must also field ground balls hit in their way, reacting quickly enough to cleanly field the ball and make precise throws to other bases or first base. Effective communication with other infielders, particularly the shortstop, is critical for ensuring appropriate positioning and effective defensive execution. To make informed decisions during plays, second basemen must have a strong awareness of the game circumstances, including the number of outs and the locations of baserunners. They must follow a variety of rules and regulations, such as achieving force outs by touching second base when receiving throws and avoiding batters and baserunners. Second base requires a combination of defensive abilities, quick reflexes, and cooperation with other infielders, making them critical contributors to the team's defense and overall effectiveness on the field.

The following are the most important characteristics of the second base position, including their responsibilities and the rules that regulate their actions:

Fielding Responsibilities

- The major task of the second baseman during defensive plays is to cover second base. They must be positioned so that they can receive throws from other infielders and tag the base to record force outs or double plays.
- **Turning Double Plays:** To complete the double play, they must receive the ball from the shortstop or other fielders, touch second base with their foot (or step on it), and make a quick, accurate throw to first base.
- **Ground Ball Fielding:** Second basemen must be capable of fielding ground balls hit in their area, both to their left and right sides. They must respond fast in order to neatly receive the ball and make accurate throws to other bases.
- **Communication and coordination:** Second basemen must successfully communicate with other infielders, particularly the shortstop, to guarantee correct positioning and efficient defensive maneuvers.
- **Fielding Ground Balls:** To make informed decisions during plays, they must have a thorough awareness

of the game scenario, including the number of outs, baserunner locations, and the score.

- **Force Outs** occur when a ground ball is hit to the first baseman or shortstop and a baserunner is forced to advance to second base. To record a force out, the second baseman must be in position to receive the throw and touch second base with their foot.
- **Tagging Runners:** If a throw to second base is delayed, the second baseman may attempt to tag the runner with the ball to record an out.
- **Interference Rules:** Second basemen must avoid interfering with the batter or impeding the paths of baserunners, as interference can result in penalties or baserunner advancement.
- **Double Play Pivot:** To complete a double play as the receiving fielder, the second baseman must pivot by stepping on second base with their foot, receiving the throw, and then throwing to first base.

Overall, the position of second base requires a combination of defensive abilities, quick reflexes, and outstanding coordination with other infielders. Their ability to read the game, communicate well, and execute defensive plays makes them vital assets to the team's on-field performance.

Third Base

In baseball, the third base position plays an important defensive role. Third basemen are key players who are responsible for patrolling the space between third base and shortstop, reacting quickly to ground balls, and making accurate throws to help the team succeed. They cover a wide defensive range, controlling hard-hit balls that come their way. They are commonly referred to as the "hot corner."

Third basemen must have a strong throwing arm to convert double plays by making lengthy throws to first base or across the diamond. They also help the shortstop and second baseman turn double plays, and field the ball cleanly. Third basemen, like other fielders, must be aware of fair and foul zones and avoid interfering with batters or impeding baserunners' paths. Their ability to handle high-speed plays, make diving stops, and respond to sharp line drives is crucial in avoiding runs by the opposing team. Third basemen are essential assets to the team's overall performance on the field since the position requires a combination of speed, quick reaction, and excellent defenses.

Fielding Responsibilities

The third baseman's major duty in the field is to catch ground balls that are batted in his direction. They need lightning-fast reactions and pinpoint accuracy to field hard-hit balls and throw out runners from other bases or from first.

- **Covering the "Hot Corner"**: Because of the high speed and hard-hit balls that come in that way, the region near third base is commonly referred to as the "hot corner." Third basemen must be ready to make difficult defensive plays and react swiftly to line drives and sharp grounders.
- **Defensive Range**: Third basemen must cover a significant amount of ground to their left and right sides, as well as handle balls hit down the foul line.
- **Throwing Arm**: A strong throwing arm is required for third basemen to make longer throws from deep in the "hot corner" to first base and across the diamond to complete double plays.
- **Turning Double Plays**: Third basemen frequently turn double plays with the shortstop and second baseman. To complete the double play, they must field the ball cleanly, step on third base (or touch it with their foot), then make quick, accurate throws to second or first base.
- **Force Outs**: When a ground ball is hit to the shortstop or second baseman and a baserunner is forced to advance to third base, the third baseman must be in position to receive the throw and touch (or step on) third base in order to record a force out.
- **Tagging Runners**: If a throw to third base is delayed, the third baseman may attempt to tag the runner with the ball to record an out.

- **Fair and Foul Territory:** Third basemen, like all fielders, must be aware of fair and foul territory and react correctly to balls hit in those areas.
- **Interference Rules:** Third basemen must avoid interfering with the batter or impeding baserunners' routes, as interference can result in penalties or baserunner advancement.

Overall, the third baseman's ability to properly field ground balls, throw accurate passes, and contribute to double plays is critical to the team's defensive performance. A talented third baseman may save runs and contribute significantly to the team's overall performance on the field.

Outfield Positions (Left Field, Center Field, and Right Field)

The outfield positions were designed to cover the huge outfield space and recover balls struck into it. Outfielders were positioned at various spots in the outfield throughout history as the game developed to provide the best coverage and prevent hits that could lead to additional bases or runs.

Left Field

In baseball, the position of left field is critical and important to the outfield. Left fielders are responsible for catching fly balls hit to the left side of the outfield as well as receiving ground balls that come their way. To make successful catches, they must have good judgment, quick reflexes, and the ability to track the direction of the ball. Left fielders, with their powerful throwing arms, also play an important part in keeping runners from advancing or attempting to score by delivering accurate and forceful throws back to the infield.

Left fielders cover a large portion of the outfield, requiring speed and agility to cover balls hit into gaps and down the left field line. Left fielders, like other fielders, must be aware of fair and foul zones and avoid interfering with hitters or disrupt the paths of baserunners. A skilled left fielder can have a large impact on the game by preventing hits, discouraging baserunners from stealing additional bases, and contributing to the team's defenses.

Fielding Responsibilities

- **Catching Fly Balls:** The left fielder's major task is to catch fly balls hit to the left side of the outfield. To make successful catches, they must have good judgment, quick reflexes, and the ability to track the direction of the ball.
- **Fielding Ground Balls:** Left fielders must be prepared to field ground balls, particularly ones hit into the left field corner.
- **Defensive Range:** Left fielders cover a large area in the outfield, thus they must be quick and have strong range to cover balls hit into the gaps and down the left field line.

Throwing Arm

Left fielders must have a strong throwing arm in order to make precise and powerful throws back to the infield, stopping runners from advancing or attempting to score.

Cut Off and Relay Plays

Left fielders frequently participate in cut-off and relay plays. When a ball is hit to right or center field, the left fielder may serve as a cut-off man, receiving the throw and passing it to the appropriate base to prevent runners from advancing.

Regulations and Rules

- **Fair and foul territory:** Left fielders, like all outfielders, must be aware of fair and foul territory and respond appropriately to balls hit in those zones.
- **Fielder's Interference:** Left fielders must avoid interfering with hitters or blocking the paths of baserunners. Interference can result in penalties or baserunner advancement.
- **Balls lost in the sun or lights:** Balls hit to the outfield can sometimes become lost in the sun or stadium lights. To make the catch, left fielders must be ready to shift their location and find the ball swiftly.

Overall, the left fielder's ability to monitor fly balls, make accurate throws, and contribute to cut-off and relay plays is critical to the defensive success of the team. A skilled left fielder can have a huge impact on the game by making difficult catches and discouraging baserunners from taking extra bases.

Center Field

The center field position in baseball is an important and challenging outfield position. Center fielders are important defensive players whose major task is to cover the widest area of the outfield, stretching from left-center to right-center field. They must have outstanding speed, agility, and range to chase down fly balls hit deep into the gaps and make tough catches. Center fielders are frequently the primary outfielders in charge of catching fly balls, which necessitates exceptional judgment and the ability to precisely assess the ball off the bat. They must also be ready to field ground balls hit into the outfield. Center fielders must have a strong and accurate throwing arm in order to make precise throws back to the infield, stopping baserunners from advancing or attempting to score. They regularly participate in cut-off and relay plays, receiving throws from other outfielders and transferring the ball to the appropriate base to prevent baserunners from advancing.

Center fielders, like all fielders, must be mindful of fair and foul zones, avoid interfering with batters, and be prepared to recover the ball quickly if it becomes lost in the sun or stadium lights. Their ability to cover a large amount of outfield ground, make difficult catches, and help to the team's defensive efforts all have a huge impact on the game's outcome. A competent center fielder can be a game-changer, avoiding runs and making game-changing plays that influence the outcome of the game.

Fielding Responsibilities

- **Covering Large Areas:** The center fielder's primary task is to cover a large amount of outfield territory ranging from left to right center field. They must have outstanding speed, agility, and range to track down fly balls struck deep into the gaps.
- **Catching Fly Balls:** Center fielders are frequently the outfielders in charge of catching fly balls. To make effective catches, they must have excellent judgment and the ability to read the ball off the bat.
- **Fielding Ground Balls:** Center fielders must be prepared to field ground balls hit into the outfield in addition to fly balls.
- **Strong Throwing Arm:** Center fielders must have a strong and accurate throwing arm in order to make accurate throws back to the infield, stopping baserunners from advancing or attempting to score.
- **Cut-off and relay duties:** Center fielders commonly participate in cut-off and relay plays. When a ball is hit to right or left field, the center fielder may serve as a cut-off player, receiving the throw and transferring it to the appropriate base in order to prevent baserunners from advancing.

- **Fair and foul territory:** Center fielders, like all outfielders, must be aware of fair and foul territory and react appropriately to balls hit in those zones.
- **Fielder's Interference:** Center fielders must avoid interfering with hitters or obstructing baserunners' routes, as interference can result in penalties or baserunner advancement.
- **Ball lost in the sun or lights:** Center fielders must be prepared to adjust their positioning and swiftly find the ball if it becomes lost in the sun or stadium lights.

The center field position necessitates a rare combination of speed, agility, and great defensive abilities. Center fielders play an important part in preventing hits and extra-base hits, making difficult catches, and contributing to the team's defensive performance. Their ability to cover a broad area of the outfield, read the ball off the bat, and make accurate throws back to the infield is critical to the team's performance. A strong center fielder may be a game changer for their team by preventing runs and making plays that affect the outcome of the game.

Right Field

In baseball, the right field position is crucial in the outfield. Right fielders are critical defensive players who cover the space between second base and the foul line in right field. Their primary task is to catch fly balls hit to the right side of the outfield, which requires sound judgment, quick reflexes, and the ability to track the ball's flight. Furthermore, right fielders must be prepared to field ground balls both in the outfield and along the right field foul line. They must cover a large area in the outfield and have the speed and range to follow down balls hit into gaps and down the right field line. Right fielders must also have a strong throwing arm in order to make accurate and powerful throws back to the infield, preventing baserunners from advancing or scoring. Cut-off and relay plays are common, with them accepting throws from other outfielders and relaying the ball to the appropriate base to prevent baserunners from advancing. Right fielders must be mindful of fair and foul territory, avoid interfering with batters, and be able to swiftly locate the ball if it becomes lost in the sun or stadium lights. Their ability to stop hits and limit runs is critical to the team's success.

Fielding Responsibilities

- **Fly Ball Catching:** The right fielder's major task is to grab fly balls hit to the right side of the outfield. To make successful catches, they must have good judgment, quick reflexes, and the ability to track the direction of the ball.
- **Fielding Ground Balls:** Right fielders must be prepared to field ground balls in the outfield as well as along the right field foul line.
- **Defensive Range:** Because right fielders are the farthest away from home plate of any outfielder, they

must cover a large area in the outfield. They must be fast and have good range to cover balls shot into gaps and down the right field line.

- Right fielders must have a strong throwing arm in order to make precise and forceful throws back to the infield, stopping baserunners from advancing or attempting to score.
- **Cut-off and relay duties:** Right fielders are frequently involved in cut-off and relay plays. When a ball is hit to center or left field, the right fielder may function as a cut-off player, receiving the throw and transferring it to the appropriate base in order to prevent baserunners from advancing.
- **Fair and Foul Territories:** Right fielders, like other outfielders, must be aware of fair and foul territory and react appropriately to balls hit in those areas.
- **Fielder's Interference:** Right fielders must avoid interfering with hitters or blocking the paths of baserunners. Interference can result in penalties or baserunner advancement.
- **Ball lost in the sun or lights:** Right fielders must be ready to fix their positioning and swiftly locate the ball if it becomes lost in the sun or stadium lights.

Right fielders are critical in minimizing runs for opposing teams. The team's defensive performance is dependent on their ability to track fly balls, field ground balls, make precise throws, and contribute to cut-off and relay plays. A strong right fielder can have a huge impact on the game by preventing runs and discouraging baserunners from taking extra bases.

When it comes to the outfield, team managers must have an awareness of each player's skill. Certain outfielders, for example, may be quicker and better suited for center field because of its bigger coverage area, whilst others with strong throwing arms may be placed in right field to make strong throws to third base or home plate.

Each player's position in baseball is like a critical puzzle piece that completes the picture of a high performing team. The pitcher sets the tone for the game with their hard deliveries. The catcher's keen vision and lightning-fast reactions keep everything in check. The first baseman, second baseman, shortstop, and third baseman all work together to protect their turf in the infield. Outfielders use their speed and precision to track down soaring hits in the outfield. Remember that every position provides an opportunity to contribute, to make incredible plays, and ultimately be a part of the team's success. So, whether you want to strike out hitters, make amazing catches, or make a great play at the plate, each position has its own distinct magic that, when combined, creates the engaging world of baseball.

Chapter 4
Famous Ballparks: Exploring the Places Where Games Happen

American ballparks have a distinct and beloved place in Major League Baseball's colorful tapestry. These legendary venues are more than simply ballfields; they are the places where legends were formed, records were broken, and unforgettable moments occurred. From the majestic Fenway Park in Boston to the magnificence of Wrigley Field in Chicago, these ballparks have watched the game's history, demonstrating its enduring appeal to generations of fans. Each ballpark's architecture and design tell their own story, reflecting the different qualities of their communities and providing an intimate connection between players and spectators. Cheers, jeers, and the crack of the bat reverberate through the decades, reminding us that these ballparks are living monuments to the energy and passion of America's sport. In this chapter, we'll explore the most legendary parks of the game.

Fenway Park

Fenway Park, the oldest ballpark in Major League Baseball, was founded on April 20, 1912 in Boston, Massachusetts. Home to the Boston Red Sox, Fenway Park has grown famous for its iconic elements throughout the course of its long history, including the "Green Monster"-- a tall left-field wall and manual scoreboard. The stadium has undergone various restorations over the years while retaining its original charm. One of the most memorable games at Fenway Park happened during Game 6 of the 1975 World Series, when the Boston Red Sox faced the Cincinnati Reds.

Carlton Fisk of the Red Sox launched a long fly ball to left field in the 12th inning in a tense and closely contested game. The ball struck the foul pole as he furiously waved his arms, resulting in a spectacular walk-off home run. Fisk's memorable celebration as he circled the bases will live on in baseball history as a symbol of the magic and drama that can occur within the walls of Fenway Park.

Fenway Park's endurance and rich history have cemented its place as a great baseball stadium. It is a treasured symbol of Boston's baseball love and an enduring monument to the sport's timeless allure.

Wrigley Field

Wrigley Field, located in Chicago, Illinois, is one of baseball's oldest ballparks, having opened its doors on April 23, 1914.

The ivy-covered outfield walls are a distinctive element of the stadium, adding to its particular appeal. Originally known as Weeghman Park, it was erected for the minor league's Chicago Whales before being renamed Cubs Park. It then became known as Wrigley Field when the Chicago Cubs took over as the major tenant in 1916. One of the most memorable moments at Wrigley Field happened during Game 3 of the 1932 World Series between the Chicago Cubs and the New York Yankees, when Babe Ruth famously called his shot before smashing a home run.

Wrigley Field's famous ivy-covered outfield walls are one of its most recognizable characteristics. During the baseball season, the outfield is decorated with thick, green ivy that creates a visually spectacular backdrop for the games. Furthermore, the stadium's hand-operated scoreboard in center field adds to its vintage appeal, representing the simplicity and romanticism of baseball's early days.

The iconic, red brick facade of Wrigley Field, as well as the famed red marquee at the main entrance, give it a distinct architectural style. With its relatively limited seating capacity, the stadium's intimate and personal feel produces an unequaled ambiance for fans, who frequently feel a deep connection to the ballpark and its history.

"The Friendly Confines" is a well-known nickname for Wrigley Field. Sportscaster Jack Brickhouse coined the phrase to characterize the pleasant and welcoming ambiance that spectators encounter when visiting Wrigley Field.

Despite the team's century-long title drought, Cubs supporters remained faithful and continued to fill the stadium with undying support and passion. Regardless of the team's performance on the field, the "Friendly Confines" became a symbol of hope, perseverance, and an unwavering love for the game.

Wrigley Field, the home of the Chicago Cubs, has seen generations of devoted supporters who have experienced both successes and misfortunes with steady devotion. The team's century-long title drought became connected with the "Curse of the Billy Goat," a legend that added to the aura and folklore surrounding the ballpark.

Wrigley Field became the center of excitement in 2016 after the Chicago Cubs ended their 108-year World Series title drought by defeating the Cleveland Indians in a dramatic Game 7. Generations of Cubs supporters who had waited a lifetime to see the team triumph at their home ballpark shed tears of joy as they witnessed the historic victory.

The ballpark has undergone several restorations and modifications throughout the years, but the Chicago Cubs organization has taken care to preserve its historic beauty and unique character. Despite the alterations, Wrigley Field is a treasured institution that maintains a particular place in the hearts of baseball fans across the country, not just in Chicago.

Wrigley Field's timeless appeal, beautiful architecture, and illustrious history have cemented its place as a great baseball stadium. It remains a revered destination for baseball fans seeking to experience the enchantment and nostalgia found only within its hallowed walls.

Yankee Stadium

The first Yankee Stadium, located in New York City's Bronx, opened its doors on April 18, 1923, earning the nickname "The House That Ruth Built." The stadium witnessed countless significant moments in baseball history while serving as the home field for the New York Yankees for nearly eight decades.

A crowd of almost 74,000 people attended the first game at Yankee Stadium on Opening Day, when the Yankees defeated their archrivals, the Boston Red Sox, 4-1. The stadium immediately developed a reputation for its prestige, seating capacity, and ability to accommodate a large number of fans.

The original Yankee Stadium was the setting for many great baseball moments. It was the home of the renowned "Murderers' Row" Yankees team of the late 1920s, which included Babe Ruth and Lou Gehrig, who dominated the league with their power hitting and helped the Yankees win numerous World Series championships.

Over the years, the stadium has undergone many modifications and extensions to meet expanding attendance and update its facilities. However, after decades of use, the original Yankee Stadium began to exhibit signs of wear and tear, requiring extensive repairs and upgrades.

The Yankees played their final game at the original Yankee Stadium on September 21, 2008, before moving to a newly constructed stadium across the street. The original stadium was closed down with a goodbye ceremony that honored the rich history and memories produced within its walls.

On April 2, 2009, the new Yankee Stadium opened just a few feet from the original location. The new stadium incorporated modern conveniences and state-of-the-art features while retaining the traditional facade and design aspects of its predecessor. It is still the home of the New York Yankees, carrying on the franchise's legacy and the history that began in the original Yankee Stadium.

Both the original and current Yankee Stadiums have been the site of innumerable iconic players, spectacular games, and unforgettable events in baseball history. It is one of the most hallowed and revered stadiums in sports, representing excellence, history, and the unrelenting devotion of Yankees supporters.

Dodger Stadium (NY & LA)

The Dodgers, Brooklyn's beloved baseball team, have been a fixture in Major League Baseball since its founding in 1876. They developed an enthusiastic and committed fan base over the years, establishing themselves as a vital part of Brooklyn's identity and culture. The team's home games were held in a variety of locations throughout the borough, with Washington Park and, later, Ebbets Field being famous symbols of Brooklyn's passion of baseball.

The Dodgers faced a big hurdle in the 1950s when their beloved home, Ebbets Field, began to show its age. Team owner Walter O'Malley envisioned a new stadium for the Dodgers that would not only meet the demands of the players but also enhance the spectator experience. He approached city officials with ideas for a new stadium in Brooklyn, but ran into barriers and opposition, resulting in a standstill in negotiations.

Frustrated by the lack of progress in getting a new stadium, O'Malley began examining alternative options, including relocating the team. The Dodgers were profoundly interwoven in the fabric of Brooklyn's history, so this concept sent shockwaves across the baseball world. Despite the team's historic links to New York, O'Malley believed that relocation to a new site was the best way for the franchise to move forward.

After considerable discussion and debate, the Brooklyn Dodgers decided to leave their home town and embark on a new adventure in Los Angeles, California, in 1957. It was a moment that would permanently alter the baseball landscape. This audacious decision marked the first time an MLB team relocated to the West Coast, and it set a precedent for future franchises to follow.

The relocation of the Dodgers to Los Angeles was welcomed with mixed feelings. While many supporters were saddened to see their club leave, others were ecstatic at the idea of a major league baseball team in their area. Los Angeles was a developing metropolis, and the entrance of the Dodgers added to the city's burgeoning status as a major sports and entertainment center.

With the relocation, the development of a new cutting-edge stadium in Los Angeles became a top priority. The groundbreaking ceremony for Dodger Stadium took place on September 17, 1959, in the scenic Chavez Ravine neighborhood. The stadium's design, led by architect Emil Praeger and engineer Raul L. Campos, focused on simplicity and outstanding views for spectators, providing fans with an unrivaled baseball experience. In the meantime, the Dodgers played their first four seasons at the Los Angeles Memorial Coliseum.

On April 10, 1962, Dodger Stadium finally opened its doors, ushering in a new era of Los Angeles Dodgers baseball on the West Coast. The opening day game versus the Cincinnati Reds was a momentous occasion, with President John F. Kennedy even throwing the ceremonial first pitch from the seats.

Dodger Stadium became identified with baseball brilliance over the years, seeing several historic events, spectacular games, and the celebration of the Dodgers' eight World Series triumphs. The stadium also hosted the MLB All-Star

Game on several occasions and became a popular location for other events such as concerts and soccer matches.

Today, Dodger Stadium remains an honor to the Dodgers' past and their journey from Brooklyn to Los Angeles. It is still regarded as an iconic emblem of the City of Angels, revered not just for its baseball heritage, but also as an architectural wonder and a renowned cultural landmark that continues to captivate spectators.

Oracle Park

Opening its gates on April 11, 2000, Oracle Park is renowned for its stunning panoramas of the San Francisco Bay and the Bay Bridge. After moving from New York to San Francisco in 1958, the San Francisco Giants made this stadium their new home. One of the most memorable games in the park's history occurred on October 21, 2012, when the Giants defeated the St. Louis Cardinals in Game 7 of the National League Championship Series to advance to the World Series, which they went on to win.

The ballpark's location near the scenic San Francisco Bay and the iconic Bay Bridge make for a very memorable baseball experience. Oracle Park has special meaning for Giants fans after the team won the World Series in 2010, 2012, and 2014.

Camden Yards

Camden Yards in Baltimore, Maryland, first welcomed fans on April 6, 1992, and is widely recognized as the catalyst for the "retro" ballpark movement. Its architecture artfully combines contemporary comforts with a throwback feel to ballparks of the early 20th century. On September 6, 1995, during a game between the Baltimore Orioles and the California Angels, Cal Ripken Jr. made history by playing in his 2,131st straight game, breaking Lou Gehrig's mark. Camden Yards is the proud home of the Baltimore Orioles.

Coors Field

On April 26, 1995, games were first played at Coors Field in Denver, Colorado. The elevated playing field is the stadium's defining characteristic, and it helps explain why so many home runs are hit there. The stadium, which bears the name of the Coors Brewing Company, whose headquarters are in neighboring Golden, Colorado, has quickly become a fan favorite. On October 1, 2007, the Colorado Rockies and the San Diego Padres played in a dramatic tiebreaker game; the Rockies won 9-8 in 13 innings to clinch their first postseason victory in franchise history. Coors Field is the home field for the Colorado Rockies.

PNC Park

Opening its doors on April 9, 2001, PNC Park in Pittsburgh, Pennsylvania, boasts breathtaking vistas of the city skyline and the Roberto Clemente Bridge along the Allegheny River. The stadium has special meaning for Pittsburgh Pirates fans because it replaced the beloved Three Rivers Stadium. On October 1, 2013, the Pittsburgh Pirates hosted their first postseason game in almost two decades, defeating the Cincinnati Reds by a score of 6-2 in the National League Wild Card Game. PNC Park is the proud home of the Pittsburgh Pirates.

Busch Stadium

The current Busch Stadium opened on April 10, 2006, in St. Louis, Missouri, replacing the original stadium, which had served as the home of the St. Louis Cardinals for nearly 40 years. The stadium's name honors the Anheuser-Busch brewing company, which has a long history in the city. On October 27, 2011, during Game 6 of the World Series between the St. Louis Cardinals and the Texas Rangers, an amazing performance occurred-- third baseman's David Freese's incredible hitting included a game-tying triple in the 9th inning and a walk-off home run in the 11th inning, sending the Cardinals to a thrilling victory and a Game 7-- which they eventually won.

Progressive Field

Progressive Field, formerly known as Jacobs Field, opened on April 4, 1994 in Cleveland, Ohio. Throughout its history as the home of the Cleveland Guardians (formerly the Cleveland Indians), the ballpark has witnessed numerous notable baseball moments. Progressive Field hosted the 1997 World Series, which pitted the Indians against the Florida Marlins in a seven-game series. The ballpark's architecture includes odd elements such as "toothbrush lights," a nod to the team's mascot. The Guardians' devoted fans make every home game a colorful and energetic experience.

Nationals Park

The opening of Nationals Park in Washington, D.C. on March 30, 2008, forever changed the city's sports environment. Nationals Park, the home of the Washington Nationals, has seen many historic baseball moments, including postseason games and huge victories. It was most recently the venue of the 2018 Major League Baseball All-Star Game, which gathered many of baseball's top stars to the nation's capital. Spectators at Nationals Park can feel like they're right on the field thanks to an innovating seating design. The ballpark also boasts scenic views of the Anacostia River.

Comerica Park

The Detroit Tigers have called Comerica Park in downtown Detroit, Michigan, their home since it opened on April 11, 2000. A statue of a ferocious tiger stands at the ballpark's main entrance, luring visitors into a venue steeped in baseball tradition. There have been many memorable games and incredible displays of skill by Tigers players at Comerica Park. It's great for families because of the welcoming environment and the many fun things to do, including riding the carousel or going on the Ferris wheel.

Baseball stadiums in America are more than just grounds; they are storied arenas where baseball stars have risen and spectacular moments have unfolded, preserving the game's history and passion for future generations of fans. In the next chapter, we'll take a deeper look at the greatest players who created memorable moments in these landmarks.

Chapter 5
Baseball Heroes: Legendary Players of the Game

Baseball legends have a distinct combination of great talent and unmatched skill that lift them above their peers. They have exceptional ability, whether it is hitting for power, demonstrating incredible speed on the basepaths, displaying defensive brilliance, or dominating on the pitcher's mound. What distinguishes them is not just their individual talents, but also their consistency in maintaining high levels of performance year after year, setting records, and sustaining success throughout a long career. Legendary players flourish in the postseason as well, delivering clutch performances at crucial moments to lead their teams to triumph in both playoff and World Series games.

Beyond their on-field accomplishments, they exemplify leadership, sportsmanship, and respect for the game, garnering appreciation from teammates and opponents alike. Their influence extends beyond the ballfield, making them cultural icons and establishing a legacy that will influence the game and society for future generations. Legendary players are not only honored throughout their careers, but they are also adored and remembered as icons of greatness long after they leave the game.

Babe Ruth

Babe Ruth, a baseball hero in the United States, was born as George Herman Ruth Jr. on February 6, 1895. Most people consider him to be among the greatest players in history. Ruth's ability to hit home runs changed the way the game was played. He was known for his tremendous strength and engaging character. During his career, which lasted from 1914 until 1935, Ruth played for both the Boston Red Sox and the New York Yankees. Ruth's outstanding accomplishments-- which included setting single-season home run records-- helped popularize baseball in the United States during the 1920s and earned him the nickname "The Sultan of Swat."

Jackie Robinson

Born on January 31, 1919, Jackie Robinson was a pioneering figure in baseball history. When he debuted for the Brooklyn Dodgers on April 15, 1947, he broke the color barrier, becoming the first African American player in contemporary Major League Baseball. Throughout his career, Robinson experienced bigotry and persecution, yet he displayed remarkable talent, courage, and dignity. His on-field achievements, as well as his crucial role in advocating racial integration in sports and society, established him as an enduring icon of civil rights and social development.

Hank Aaron

Hank Henry Louis "Hank" Aaron Jr. Aaron, who was born on February 5, 1934, was a baseball great noted for his outstanding hitting and career longevity. Nicknamed "Hammerin' Hank," Aaron played 23 seasons in Major League Baseball, principally with the Milwaukee Brewers and Atlanta Braves. For more than three decades, he held the all-time home run record, surpassing Babe Ruth's mark, and concluded his career with 755 home runs. Aaron's poise, steadiness, and contributions to the game gained him a great deal of respect and appreciation.

Willie Mays

Willie Howard Mays Jr., born on May 6, 1931, was one of baseball's most skilled players. Mays is known for his remarkable abilities at the plate and in the outfield. He spent 22 seasons in Major League Baseball, mostly with the New York/San Francisco Giants and the New York Mets. Mays' athleticism, defensive prowess, and offensive genius helped him become a sports icon and a role model for future generations of players. Winning the National League MVP twice, his records include 338 stolen bases and 2000 runs scored throughout his career.

Ted Williams

Born on August 30, 1918, Ted Williams was a professional baseball player known for his powerful swing. A left-handed slugger, Williams spent his entire career with the Boston Red Sox. Earning the nicknames "The Splendid Splinter" and "Teddy Ballgame," Williams won the Triple Crown twice and is the last player in major league history to hit .400 in a single season. Ted Williams is widely regarded as one of baseball's all-time greatest batters—owing to his powerful command of the bat and strike zone.

Cy Young

Cy Young, real name Denton True Young, was born on March 29, 1867, and he became a legendary baseball pitcher for the American league. From 1890 until 1911, he was a fixture in Major League Baseball and set an unbreakable record for 511 career wins. Young threw three no-hitters and is still in the top ten all-time in strikeouts, shutouts and pitched innings. He was revered for his strong fastball, perfect control, and good sportsmanship. The Cy Young Award, presented to baseball's greatest pitcher each year since 1956, was named after him. In 1937, he was recognized as one of baseball's all-time greats and inducted into the Baseball Hall of Fame.

Lou Gehrig

Legendary New York Yankees first baseman Lou Gehrig was born on June 19, 1903. The record 2,130 straight games played by "The Iron Horse" Lou Gehrig remained for decades. Because of his strong hitting and reliable play, he was an integral part of the Yankees' championship teams of the 1920s and 1930s. A career .340 batting average, 493 home runs, and 1,995 RBIs are just some of Gehrig's outstanding career statistics. His longevity and record-setting 2,130-game endured for decades before it was surpassed. The tragic end to Gehrig's career was brought about by his diagnosis with amyotrophic lateral sclerosis, most generally known as "Lou Gehrig's disease." His final address at Yankee Stadium in 1939, in which he called himself "the luckiest man on the face of the earth," is widely regarded as one of the most touching moments in sports history. One of baseball's all-time greats, Gehrig was praised for his skill and integrity both on and off the field.

Roberto Clemente

Roberto Clemente was an outfielder with the Pittsburgh Pirates who was born on August 18, 1934 and went by the name Roberto Clemente Walker. Clemente was a powerful hitter in addition to his reputation as a great defensive player. In 1971, he made history as the first Latin American player to be named World Series MVP, and he went on to win 12 Gold Gloves throughout his career. Clemente was also deeply committed to helping others off the field, and he sadly died on his way to offer aid to earthquake victims in Nicaragua on December 31, 1972. Beyond baseball, he will be remembered for encouraging future generations to make a difference in the world by giving back to their communities.

Satchel Paige

One of baseball's most entertaining and talented pitchers, Leroy Robert "Satchel" Paige was born on July 7, 1906. Since MLB was still segregated at the time, Paige spent much of his career in the segregated leagues. In 1948, at the age of 42, Paige became the oldest MLB rookie when he signed with the Cleveland Indians. Well-known for his charisma and exceptional pitching skills, Paige was an important element of the Indians' pitching rotation. He possessed an extensive arsenal of pitches, as well as a distinct pitching technique, that disoriented opposing batters. Paige was a feared opponent on the mound due to his superb control, unconventional windup, and blistering fastball. Satchel Paige was instrumental in the Indians winning the American League pennant in 1948-- the same year he joined the organization. His contributions to the team's victory were acknowledged as he became the first African-American pitcher to appear in a World Series game. Paige was inducted into the Baseball Hall of Fame in 1971 in recognition of his extraordinary talent and his efforts to advance racial equality in the sport.

Sandy Koufax

Sanford Koufax, nicknamed "Sandy Koufax," was a left-handed pitcher for the Brooklyn/Los Angeles Dodgers from 1955 to 1966. Koufax won three Cy Young Awards and five straight ERA crowns due to his extraordinary talent and dominance on the mound. He had a remarkable run of success in the 1960s that has led many to call him one of the best pitchers in MLB history. Koufax's legendary standing in baseball was cemented by his incredible postseason exploits, which included four no-hitters and a perfect game.

Ty Cobb

Ty Cobb, born on December 18, 1886, was one of the Dead Ball Era's most aggressive and skilled players. Cobb's playing style and accomplishments earned him the moniker "The Georgia Peach." He was a hard competitor and aggressive baserunner. He primarily played for the Detroit Tigers, where he set hitting and stolen base records. Cobb's .366 lifetime batting average is still the highest in MLB history.

Stan Musial

Stanley Musial was a renowned outfielder and first baseman who spent his whole 22-season career with the St. Louis Cardinals. Musial, sometimes known as "Stan the Man," was a reliable batter and three-time MVP. He established himself as one of baseball's all-time greats, concluding his career with 3,630 hits and countless awards for his contributions to the game.

Mickey Mantle

Mickey Mantle was a legendary switch-hitting outfielder who spent his entire 18-year career with the New York Yankees. He was born on October 20, 1931. Mantle was recognized for his incredible strength and speed, giving him the moniker "The Commerce Comet." He won three MVP awards and was instrumental in the Yankees' success in the 1950s and 1960s. Despite repeated injuries, Mantle remains a living emblem of baseball greatness.

Nolan Ryan

Nolan, Lynn Ryan Nolan Ryan Jr., born on January 31, 1947, was a dominating pitcher in major league baseball. Ryan's blistering fastball and stamina on the mound earned him the nickname "The Ryan Express." He set multiple records, including the most career strikeouts-- 5,714-- and the most no-hitters, totaling seven games. His hard ethic and competitiveness helped him become a baseball legend.

Derek Jeter

Derek Sanderson Jeter, who was born on June 26, 1974, was the New York Yankees' captain and shortstop for two decades. During the Yankees' remarkable run in the late

1990s and early 2000s-- during which they won five World Series-- Derek Jeter was the face of the team. He was renowned for his leadership, critical performances, and exceptional defensive abilities. His professionalism and accomplishments off the field have further cemented his status as one of baseball's finest players.

Cal Ripken Jr

Born on August 24, 1960, Calvin Edwin Ripken Jr. is most known for his incredible consecutive games played streak, which reached a record-breaking 2,632 games. Ripken, a gifted shortstop and third baseman, spent his entire 21-year career with the Baltimore Orioles. "The Iron Man" represented perseverance and was widely considered as one of the game's most renowned ambassadors.

Ken Griffey Jr

Born on November 21, 1969, Ken Griffey Jr. was a powerful outfielder with a clean swing and great defensive ability. Griffey played for the Seattle Mariners and the Cincinnati Reds for the most of his career. Nicknamed "The Kid", Griffey was an electric athlete who charmed spectators with his talent and upbeat demeanor on the field. He was well recognized for his signature backward cap and rose to prominence as one of baseball's top stars in the 1990s.

Mariano Rivera

Born on November 29, 1969, Mariano Rivera became baseball's greatest closer. Famous for his deadly "cutter," Rivera threw exclusively for the New York Yankees during the course of his 19-year professional career. He was known as "The Sandman" due to his constant performance under intense duress and postseason excellence. With his poise and precision in the ninth inning, Rivera became a fan favorite and an integral part of the Yankees' success.

Joe DiMaggio

Famous center fielder Joe DiMaggio was born on November 25, 1914, and was nicknamed "The Yankee Clipper." Famous for his smooth swing and powerful hitting, DiMaggio spent his whole 13-year career with the New York Yankees. His amazing 1941 hitting streak of 56 games is still one of baseball's all-time best marks. DiMaggio was one of the most revered individuals in 20th century baseball because of his accomplishments and iconic stature.

Greg Maddux

Gregory Alan Maddux was a legendary pitcher known for his command and precision. During his time with the Chicago Cubs and the Atlanta Braves when he won four consecutive Cy Young Awards from 1992 to 1995, Maddux was a dominant pitcher. One of the best pitchers of his era, thanks to his perfect location and analytical approach to the game.

Albert Pujols

Jose Alberto Pujols Alcántara, better known as Albert Pujols, was born on January 16, 1980, and is a Dominican-American first baseman who is widely considered to be one of the best hitters of all time. During his meteoric rise with the St. Louis Cardinals, Pujols won two World Series rings and three MVP honors. The combination of his strength and reliability as a batter gave him the moniker "The Machine." With more than 3,000 hits and 600 home runs, Albert Pujols has established himself as one of baseball's all-time greats.

Each of these players has made an unforgettable mark on the sport of baseball, having an impact not only on the history and culture of the game-- but also on future generations of players and fans.

Chapter 6
The Greatest Teams That Ruled the Field

Creating a legendary baseball team involves a number of important factors to make the lineup truly iconic and unforgettable. At the heart of the team is outstanding talent and skill, with players that excel in multiple aspects of the game, including hitting, pitching, fielding, and baserunning. A legendary team also has depth and balance, with both star players and a dependable offense who can contribute successfully in multiple situations. Veteran players or coaches must inspire and guide the team while also establishing a sense of unity and purpose. Furthermore, successful teams have exceptional chemistry and friendship, with players supporting and uplifting one another. Overcoming obstacles is a distinguishing feature of legendary teams, demonstrating their resilience in the face of adversity and their capacity to rise to the moment. They set records and leave an unmistakable mark on the game.

They are teams that shine in memorable games, becoming part of baseball history and ingrained in the hearts of fans. A remarkable team's legacy endures, continuing to be honored and remembered as icons of greatness.

Choosing the greatest baseball teams in history is subjective as opinions differ based on personal tastes and historical viewpoints. In this chapter we'll take a deeper look at iconic teams and their respective seasons that are frequently regarded as among the finest due to their extraordinary performance, ability to overcome hurdles, and noteworthy games.

1927 New York Yankees

The 1927 Yankees, dubbed "Murderers' Row," were a dominating force in baseball history. The team, led by Babe Ruth and Lou Gehrig, went 110-44 during the regular season and swept the Pittsburgh Pirates in the World Series. Their lineup was loaded with Hall of Famers, and they established a level of brilliance that is still held in high regard today.

The Yankees faced difficulties and defeats in the early 1920s. The team had shown potential after obtaining Babe Ruth from the Boston Red Sox in 1919, but had yet to win a World Series. However, by the mid-1920s, the Yankees' fortunes began to improve as they assembled a powerful lineup centered on Ruth, Gehrig, and other great players.

The 1927 Yankees had an extraordinarily strong offensive that earned them the moniker "Murderers' Row" due to their ability to destroy opposing pitchers. Ruth, dubbed the "Sultan of Swat," set a single-season record with 60 home runs, which stood for decades. The "Iron Horse," Lou Gehrig, was just as spectacular, hitting .373 hits, 47 home runs, and 175 RBIs.

The Yankees also boasted excellent hitters such as Earle Combs, Bob Meusel, Tony Lazzeri, and Mark Koenig-- producing a batting order that frightened any pitcher on the mound.

During the regular season, the 1927 Yankees dominated, finishing with a record of 110 wins and 44 losses-- claiming the American League pennant by a large margin. They were led by manager Miller Huggins, who controlled the lineup and pitching staff expertly.

That year, the Yankees met the reigning champion Pittsburgh Pirates in the World Series. Despite being a formidable foe, the Pirates were no match for the Yankees' offensive prowess. Sweeping the Pirates in four games, the Yankees won the World Series.

The Yankees' victory in 1927 cemented their position in history. Their strong lineup and dominance on the field set records and set a new bar for baseball brilliance.

1939 New York Yankees

Another iconic Yankees team, the 1939 roster, is often praised for their impressive 106-45 regular-season record and a World Series victory over the Cincinnati Reds.

Managed by Joe McCarthy, the New York Yankees of 1939 were a baseball powerhouse that continued the team's tradition of excellence and success.

In the early 1930s, the Yankees experienced a few seasons without a World Series title after their dominance in the late 1920s. However, by the late 1930s, the team once again became a formidable force.

The 1939 Yankees boasted an impressive lineup that included future Hall of Famers such as Joe DiMaggio, Bill Dickey, and Red Ruffing. DiMaggio, known as the "Yankee Clipper," was the team's star center fielder and an offensive powerhouse. Dickey was a skilled catcher, and Ruffing led the pitching staff with his impressive performances on the mound.

During the 1939 regular season, the Yankees played consistently well, finishing with a record of 106 wins and 45 losses. They were dominant in the American League, securing the pennant with ease.

In the World Series, the Yankees faced the Cincinnati Reds, who had also enjoyed a successful season. Despite the Reds' competitive spirit, the Yankees' talent and experience proved too much to handle. In a decisive series, the Yankees emerged as the victors, defeating the Reds in four games.

In 1939, the Yankees won the World Series and established themselves as one of baseball's all-time greatest teams. Being the fourth World Series win in a row, the team established themselves as a dynasty, with their triumph being the collective result of many players.

The achievements of the 1939 Yankees are still celebrated today-- with the ups and downs they experienced that year being a testament to the team's resilience to remain a major league powerhouse.

1955 Brooklyn Dodgers

In 1955, the Dodgers beat the Yankees and won the World Series for the first time in franchise history. Overcoming years of disappointment, this lineup led by Jackie Robinson, Duke Snider, and Roy Campanella eventually won a series title for Brooklyn.

When the 1955 baseball season began, the Brooklyn Dodgers became known as the "Boys of Summer." The Dodgers were a team full of talent and determination, guided by their adored manager, Walter Alston.

The Dodgers encountered many challenges on their way to the 1955 World Series. As the 1950s progressed, the Dodgers continued to fall up short in their pursuit of a World Series championship. They were notorious rivals of the New York

Yankees, with whom they met repeatedly in the World Series but were always defeated.

The 1955 season, however, was a different story. The Dodgers showed tremendous fortitude and consistency all season long, winning the National League title with a record of 98-55.

In addition to Jackie Robinson, Roy Campanella, Duke Snider, Pee Wee Reese, and Gil Hodges, the Dodgers lineup was stacked with several future Hall of Famers. Robinson was the first African-American to play in Major League Baseball, and he was more than simply a pioneer; he was also a tremendously influential player at second base. Campanella, the Dodgers' catcher, was both a slugger and a key cog in the team's pitching machine.

In 1955, the Dodgers and the Yankees met again in the World Series. Despite the Dodgers' postseason dominance, the Yankees were able to defeat them in the World Series.

However, the Dodgers were determined to learn from their errors and develop. Over the span of seven games, they displayed extraordinary skill. Both teams were extremely aggressive, and the match was tight.

The Dodgers ultimately claimed the World Series by defeating the Yankees 2-0 in Game 7 of the series. The victory was secured by the outstanding performance of adolescent left-handed pitcher Johnny Podres. Brooklyn was ecstatic to commemorate the Dodgers' first World Series victory since the formation of the team in 1884.

In baseball's racially segregated world, the 1955 World Series victory by the Brooklyn Dodgers represented a symbol of optimism and change to their devoted fan base. More than just a baseball victory, the team's victory represented growth and unity.

Many baseball enthusiasts continue to refer to the 1955 Dodgers as the "Boys of Summer" due to their phenomenal season. Their struggles and ultimate success represent tenacity and the efficacy of teamwork. Their victory was a cornerstone of the legendary past of the Brooklyn Dodgers and has inspired baseball enthusiasts for decades.

1975 Cincinnati Reds

The 1975 Reds, dubbed the "Big Red Machine," dominated the regular season with a 108-54 record. They had an impressive lineup that included Pete Rose, Johnny Bench, Joe Morgan, and Tony Perez. They defeated the Boston Red Sox in seven games in one of the most memorable World Series, with Game 6 being an all-time classic.

The Cincinnati Reds of 1975 were a baseball club that exemplified tenacity and perseverance. The Reds were a force to be reckoned with in the National League, led by their legendary manager, Sparky Anderson.

The Reds' path to the 1975 World Series was not without difficulties. The club had suffered multiple setbacks and near-misses in the years preceding up to the 1975 season. In 1970, they reached the World Series but were defeated by the Baltimore Orioles. The disappointment of prior years' failures served as a motivator for the Reds to work harder and achieve success this year.

The Reds' amazing consistency and dominance defined the 1975 season. They concluded the regular season with an outstanding 108-win-54-loss record, earning the National League pennant and establishing themselves as the team to beat.

Stars like Johnny Bench, Pete Rose, Joe Morgan, Tony Perez, and Dave Concepción populated the Reds' roster. Bench was a fantastic catcher and a power hitter, and Morgan was an important offensive and defensive player at second base. Pete Rose, nicknamed "Charlie Hustle," was the team's driving force thanks to his typical tenacity and adaptability.

The 1975 World Series featured the Reds and the Boston Red Sox, two teams with championship aspirations of their own. The series was hotly contested, with intensity from both teams.

In the eighth inning of Game 6 of the World Series, the Reds were down by three runs. A three-run homer by Bench and a game-winning single by Rose in the ninth inning helped them come back and force a crucial Game 7.

The Reds won the World Series for the first time since 1940 due to their outstanding collaboration and dedication in Game 7, where they prevailed 4-3. Morgan's game-winning single in the ninth inning was the deciding factor, giving the Reds the championship.

The 1975 World Series victory by the Cincinnati Reds was cause for jubilation among the team's legion of committed followers. It was the climax of years of effort and sacrifice, forever cementing the Reds' place as one of baseball's most powerful teams.

The 1975 Reds' victory and resiliency continue to motivate baseball fans, serving as a reminder of the value of dedication and cooperation on the path to success. Their triumph is still remembered as a watershed moment in MLB history and will live on in the record books of the legendary Cincinnati Reds.

1998 New York Yankees

The 1998 Yankees were unstoppable, as seen by their 114-win regular season record and mere 48-loss record. They had a formidable pitching staff and a roster that included players like Derek Jeter, Bernie Williams, and Paul O'Neill. A perfect performance in the World Series against the San Diego Padres capped off a great year for the team.

Under Joe Torre's leadership, the 1998 New York Yankees were a dominant force in Major League Baseball, displaying unprecedented levels of individual skill and collective brilliance.

The Yankees have been having difficulty in recent years before to the 1998 season. Despite being a competitive team year in and year out, they had failed to win the World Series since 1996. But that only made them more resolved to get the title back.

The Yankees' outstanding regular-season performance in 1998 was a hallmark of the season. With a final record of 114 wins and only 48 defeats, they established a new single-season record for victories in the American League. Stellar players like Derek Jeter, Bernie Williams, Paul O'Neill, and Tino Martinez anchored the team's lineup. Their pitching staff was also strong, with stars like Andy Pettitte, David Cone, and Mariano Rivera at the helm.

The Yankees' supremacy in the American League was on full display as they cruised to a regular season championship. In Game 1 of the 1998 World Series, the Yankees met the San Diego Padres, who were making their first World Series appearance since 1984. The Padres fought valiantly despite being the underdog—however, the Yankees' superior talent and experience ultimately won out.

The Yankees won the World Series for the 24th time in a stunning four-game sweep. The pitching staff was the team's ace, as they limited the Padres' formidable offense to only six runs for the whole series.

For the die-hard New York Yankees fan base, the team's 1998 World Series victory was a cause for celebration. It was the crowning achievement of a historic season that forever established them as one of baseball's all-time best teams.

A reminder of the value of skill, teamwork, and determination, the 1998 Yankees' domination and accomplishments are still held in high regard by baseball fans today. A monument to the strength of a unified and skilled lineup aiming for excellence, their epic season will forever be a part of the New York Yankees' legendary history.

1906 Chicago Cubs

The 1906 Chicago Cubs set a new standard for success in Major League Baseball by finishing the regular season with a record of 116 wins and only 36 losses. They were a well-rounded team led by manager Frank Chance and made it all the way to the World Series, before losing to their crosstown rivals, the Chicago White Sox.

The Cubs had been through some rough times in the years leading up to the 1906 season. In 1903 and 1905, they advanced to the World Series before ultimately losing. Despite their regular-season success, the Cubs craved a championship.

In 1906, the Cubs were remarkably stable and dominant. During the regular season, they went on an incredible run that resulted in 116 victories and only 36 defeats. Prominent players such as Joe Tinker, Johnny Evers, Frank Chance, and Mordecai "Three Finger" Brown populated the roster.

The Cubs had one of the strongest pitching staffs in the league due to "Three Finger" Brown, whose unconventional delivery baffled hitters. Because of their remarkable steadiness throughout the season, the 1906 Chicago Cubs won the National League title. The Cubs next faced their fierce rivals in the 1906 World Series-- the Chicago White Sox. The Cubs wanted to end their own championship drought and they ultimately defeated the White Sox in a thrilling and long World Series-- taking the series in six games. Limiting the White Sox's strong offense was the key to the Cubs' success.

When the Chicago Cubs won the World Series in 1906, their fans rejoiced. It was the climax of a remarkable season and cemented their place in baseball lore as one of the all-time great teams. Their historic 1906 season serves as a constant reminder of the power of skill, teamwork, and persistence.

1995 Atlanta Braves

The 1995 Atlanta Braves had one of the most dominant pitching rotations in baseball history, led by Greg Maddux, Tom Glavine, and John Smoltz. They won 90 games during the regular season and overcame a 3-1 deficit in the National League Championship Series to reach the World Series-- where they defeated the Cleveland Indians in six games.

The Atlanta Braves of 1995 were a tough and determined team that overcame hardship to become a major league baseball powerhouse. Managed by Bobby Cox, the Braves boasted outstanding talent and a deep roster.

The Braves had some difficulties in the years preceding the 1995 season. Despite being a strong force in the National League throughout the early 1990s and winning many division titles, they had experienced postseason heartbreak--falling short of a World Series title.

The Braves' determination and perseverance defined the 1995 season. They won the National League East by finishing the regular season with a record of 90 wins and 54 defeats. Chipper Jones, Greg Maddux, Tom Glavine, John Smoltz, and David Justice were among the many all-stars on the Braves' roster. In 1995, rookie of the year Chipper Jones significantly boosted the team's offense, while the power trio of Greg Maddux, Tom Glavine, and John Smoltz kept opposing hitters at bay.

In the 1995 National League Championship Series, the Atlanta Braves confronted the Cincinnati Reds, a formidable opponent. The Braves overcame a 2-0 series deficit to win four consecutive games and advance to the Fall Classic. Atlanta and Cleveland faced off in the 1995 World Series, with both teams attempting to claim their first championship since 1948. Throughout the entire series, both teams engaged in a fierce rivalry.

After a thrilling six-game series, the Braves carried home their first championship trophy since relocating to Atlanta. Tom Glavine's spectacular Game 6 performance, in which he pitched a one-hit shutout, determined the series.

Atlanta Braves fans were elated after their team won the World Series in 1995. It was the culmination of years of hard work and sacrifice, establishing the Braves as one of baseball's elite teams for all time.

1912 Boston Red Sox

With Babe Ruth at the helm as a teenage pitcher, the 1912 Red Sox won 105 games during the regular season and the World Series in a thrilling eight-game series against the New York Giants and the famous Christy Mathewson.

The 1912 Boston Red Sox were a strong team that had its ups and downs on the field. With Jake Stahl as manager, the Red Sox were hungry to make their mark in baseball's highest league. There had been rough times for the Red Sox in the years running up to 1912. They had come close to winning the World Series before, but had ultimately fallen short. The 1912 season, however, provided the team with a chance to prove what they were capable of.

Star players such as Tris Speaker, Duffy Lewis, and Smoky Joe Wood were featured on the 1912 Red Sox roster. The team's offense relied heavily on Tris Speaker, an outstanding outfielder, and Smoky Joe Wood, a powerful pitcher who led the league in victories and scored run average.

The Red Sox played in a tough American League division all season. However, they had a record of 105 wins and 47 loses despite several ups and downs-- good enough to win the American League title.

The Red Sox next faced off against the New York Giants in the 1912 World Series. The series was fiercely fought and the Red Sox won their second World Series after eight thrilling games. Smoky Joe Wood's brilliant pitching exploits were the series' highlights, especially his shutout pitches in Game 8 that clinched the championship for the Red Sox.

1970 Baltimore Orioles

Brooks Robinson, Frank Robinson, and Jim Palmer were among the talents on the 1970 Orioles roster. They won 108 games throughout the regular season and swept the Cincinnati Reds in the World Series, demonstrating their superiority.

The 1970 Baltimore Orioles were a spectacular club that had both troubles and successes during the season. The Orioles sought to build on their recent triumphs and win another World Series title under manager Earl Weaver.

The Orioles had established themselves as a competitive force in Major League Baseball in the years leading up to the 1970 season. In 1966, they reached the World Series but were defeated by the Los Angeles Dodgers. The team was adamant about returning to the Fall Classic and winning the championship.

Brooks Robinson, recognized for his outstanding defensive abilities at third base, was also a powerful hitter. That season, Frank Robinson, the team's skipper and offensive juggernaut, was selected the American League MVP. The Orioles were challenged all season long by strong competition from American League rivals. However, the team's 108 victories and 54 losses over the course of the season was enough to secure them the American League pennant.

The pitching staff of the Orioles, led by Jim Palmer, was one of the strongest in the league. Palmer's outstanding performances on the mound proved critical to the team's win. In the 1970 World Series, the Orioles faced off against a talented and very determined Cincinnati Reds roster.

After sweeping the Reds in a five-game series, the Orioles won the World Series-- highlighted by Brooks Robinson's stellar defensive play and Frank Robinson's excellent hitting. Years of dedication paid off, as the Orioles secured their place in baseball history as a dominant force.

To this day, baseball fans still pay tribute to the 1970 Orioles, whose grit and success serve as a reminder of the value of teamwork and dedication.

2004 Boston Red Sox

The 2004 Red Sox staged one of baseball's most incredible comebacks. In the American League Championship Series against the New York Yankees, they were down 3-0 before winning the next four games to get to the World Series.

In 2004, the Boston Red Sox set out to end the fabled "Curse of the Bambino"— an 86 year championship drought. The Red Sox, led by Terry Francona, were desperate to win the World Series.

The team had endured decades of hardship and grief, especially at the hands of their archrivals the New York Yankees, prior to the 2004 season. Many times they had been close to winning the World Series, but had ultimately fallen short.

In 2004, Pedro Martinez, Manny Ramirez, David Ortiz, and Curt Schilling were just some of the notable players on the Red Sox's formidable roster. Manny Ramirez and David Ortiz were offensive juggernauts, and Pedro Martinez dominated on the mound.

The Red Sox displayed resiliency and resolve throughout the course of the regular season. They overcame obstacles in the postseason and proved their determination and team unity by winning the American League Championship Series.

The Red Sox next met the Cardinals in the 2004 World Series. The series was a heated match, but the Red Sox were able to maintain their winning streak due to their strong offense and solid pitching.

In a thrilling four-game sweep, the Red Sox won the World Series, overcoming the "Curse of the Bambino" and ending a lengthy championship drought. Curt Schilling's legendary "bloody sock" performance in Game 6 of the World Series clinched the victory and championship for the Red Sox.

The victory of the Boston Red Sox in the 2004 World Series was cause for celebration among the team's legion of devoted supporters. It put an end to years of frustration and disappointment and cemented their status as a legendary baseball team.

1976 Cincinnati Reds

The 1976 Cincinnati Reds, nicknamed the "Big Red Machine," were a formidable club. They won the World Series by defeating the New York Yankees after finishing the regular season with a 102-60 record. The Reds, led by superstars such as Joe Morgan, Johnny Bench, and Pete Rose-- displayed a formidable lineup and pitching staff, solidifying their position as one of the greatest teams in Major League Baseball history. The Reds, led by manager Sparky Anderson, intended to expand on their previous success and establish themselves as a major league baseball powerhouse.

In the years leading up to the 1976 season, the Reds were a consistently competitive team, reaching the postseason every year. In 1970, they were defeated by the Baltimore Orioles in the World Series by a single game. However, the 1976 season afforded the team with a chance to achieve its ultimate goal.

Throughout the regular season, the Reds had competition from other strong National League teams. Despite several ups and downs, they showed perseverance and consistency to win the National League pennant with a record of 102 wins and 60 defeats.

The Reds fortuitously met the defending champions, the New York Yankees, in the 1976 World Series. Even though the Yankees were a difficult foe, the Reds were determined to win their first World Series since 1940.

And as fate would have it, the Reds ultimately defeated the Yankees in a four-game sweep to win their first World Series title in 36 years. The series itself was highlighted by the Reds' excellent offensive and defensive performances. Johnny Bench was voted World Series MVP.

The victory of the Cincinnati Reds in 1976 was a moment of triumph and celebration for their ardent fan base. It was the culmination of years of hard work and effort, cementing the Reds' legacy as one of baseball's most powerful teams.

1948 Cleveland Indians

The 1948 Indians were a tough team that overcame hardship to win the World Series. They finished the regular season with a 97-58 record, headed by players such as Bob Feller,

Lou Boudreau, and Larry Doby. In the World Series, they defeated the Boston Braves in a thrilling six-game contest. The Cleveland Indians of 1948 had both troubles and wins during this season. The Indians, led by Lou Boudreau, were determined to build on their prior accomplishments and win the World Series.

The Indians had been a competitive team in the years leading up to the 1948 season, finishing towards the top of the American League standings. However, they had not won a World Series title since 1920, and the 1948 season gave an opportunity to end their championship drought.

The 1948 Indians had a talented lineup that included talents like as Bob Feller, Larry Doby, and Lou Boudreau. Bob Feller, nicknamed "Rapid Robert," was one of baseball's most dominant pitchers, while Larry Doby was the American League's first African-American player and a tremendous batter. The player-manager, Lou Boudreau, was a skilled infielder and a major leader on and off the field.

Throughout the regular season, the Indians were tested by other strong American League teams. Despite numerous ups and downs, they displayed perseverance and consistency, finishing with a record of 97 wins and 58 losses-- capturing the American League pennant. The Indians next played the Boston Braves in the 1948 World Series. Even though the Braves were a talented and competitive team, the Indians were anxious to win their first World Series triumph in over three decades.

The World Series was a hard fought battle, with both teams putting on their finest displays. The Indians won their second World Series title, defeating the Braves in a thrilling six-game series. The series was highlighted by Gene Bearden's great pitching performances, including a complete-game shutout in Game 3 and a save in Game 6 to win the Indians' triumph.

The victory of the Cleveland Indians in 1948 was the culmination of years of hard work and sacrifice, cementing the Indians' position as one of the most recognized teams in baseball history.

1969 New York Mets

The 1969 Mets pulled off one of baseball's most incredible comebacks. After years of mediocrity, they improved to a 100-62 regular-season record under manager Gil Hodges. In the World Series, they defeated the strongly favored Baltimore Orioles in five games to win their first title.

The Mets had been one of the league's struggling clubs in the years preceding the 1969 season. They had consistently ended around the bottom of the standings since its start in 1962. The 1969 season, on the other hand, provided an opportunity for the Mets to demonstrate their potential and turn their fortunes around.

The 1969 Mets had a talented team that included Tom Seaver, Jerry Koosman, Cleon Jones, and Tommie Agee. Tom

Seaver, nicknamed "Tom Terrific," was the team's ace pitcher and a formidable force on the mound. Jerry Koosman was another dependable pitcher, and Cleon Jones and Tommie Agee contributed significantly on offense.

Throughout the regular season, the Mets had competition from other good National League teams. Despite several ups and downs, they showed tenacity and commitment to win the National League East with a record of 100 wins and 62 loses. The Mets met the Atlanta Braves in the 1969 National League Championship Series, where they triumphed due to their tenacity and outstanding pitching efforts-- earning the team a spot in the World Series.

The Mets played the powerful Baltimore Orioles in the 1969 World Series. The defending champions, the Baltimore Orioles, were heavy favorites to win. The Mets, on the contrary, proceeded to defy the odds by putting on a brilliant display of offense and defense.

The Mets won their first World Series title in team history, defeating the Orioles in a thrilling five-game battle. Tom Seaver's superb pitching outings and the team's strong defensive play were highlights of the series. The New York Mets victory in 1969 cementing their legacy as one of baseball's most famous underdog stories.

1929 Philadelphia Athletics

The Athletics of 1929 were a dominant team managed by Connie Mack. They finished the regular season with a 104-46 record due to the talents of players like Lefty Grove, Mickey Cochrane, and Jimmie Foxx. They won their second consecutive World Series after defeating the Chicago Cubs in five games.

The 1929 Philadelphia Athletics were a formidable club that endured both troubles and spectacular successes throughout the season. The Athletics had established themselves as one of Major League Baseball's dominant teams in the years leading up to the 1929 season. They had previously won the World Series in 1910, 1911, and 1913, and the 1929 season provided an opportunity to restore championship glory.

Lefty Grove was a strong pitcher, while Jimmie Foxx and Al Simmons were powerful hitters who created a fearsome offensive tandem. Mickey Cochrane was a talented catcher and an important team leader.

Throughout the regular season, the Athletics had competition from other good American League teams. Despite several ups and downs, they showed perseverance and consistency to win the American League pennant with a record of 104 wins and 46 defeats.

The Athletics met the Chicago Cubs in the 1929 World Series. The Cubs were determined to win their first World

Series since 1908, while the Athletics wanted to add another victory to their illustrious history.

Lefty Grove's tremendous pitching performances, as well as Jimmie Foxx and Al Simmons' offensive skills, were highlights of the series. Connie Mack's great team play and leadership were critical elements in the Athletics' victory.

The World Series was a tightly fought struggle in which both teams gave their best performances. Ultimately, the Athletics defeated the Cubs in a thrilling five-game series to win their fifth World Series title in franchise history.

Their momentous success is an enduring part of the Philadelphia Athletics' illustrious history, and it stands as a testament to the force of talent and tenacity in overcoming the rigors of the game.

2001 Arizona Diamondbacks

The Diamondbacks were a fledgling franchise in 2001, but they rapidly established themselves as a competitive team. They finished the season with a 92-70 record and a powerful pitching staff headed by Randy Johnson and Curt Schilling. They met the New York Yankees in the World Series and won in seven games, with Luis Gonzalez's walk-off single in Game 7 becoming a famous event in baseball history. The Diamondbacks, managed by Bob Brenly, hoped to build a name for themselves in the league and achieve success in their fourth season.

The Diamondbacks had shown promise and progressively improved in the years preceding up to the 2001 season. However, they had not yet achieved substantial postseason success, and the 2001 season provided an opportunity for them to do so.

Randy Johnson and Curt Schilling were great pitchers who formed a strong top-of-the-rotation combo. Luis Gonzalez and Matt Williams were important offensive players, offering power and consistency at the plate. The Diamondbacks faced tough competition in the National League during the regular season. However, they had shown tenacity and commitment in winning the National League West with a record of 92 wins and 70 loses.

The Arizona Diamondbacks met the Atlanta Braves in the 2001 National League Championship Series. The series was hotly contested, but the Diamondbacks showed their talent and tenacity to win-- earning their first trip to the World Series.

The Diamondbacks next played the legendary New York Yankees in the 2001 World Series, who were attempting to win their fourth consecutive crown. The World Series was one of the most dramatic in history, with both teams putting on their greatest performances.

Ultimately, the Diamondbacks won their first World Series title in team history, defeating the Yankees in a thrilling seven-game series. The series was highlighted by Luis Gonzalez's stunning walk-off single in the bottom of the ninth inning of Game 7, which secured the Diamondbacks' triumph.

The victory of the Arizona Diamondbacks in 2001 was a moment of triumph and celebration for their ardent fan base.

All American Girls Professional Baseball

During World War II, the All-American Girls Professional Baseball League was a new and trailblazing venture that aimed to give women the opportunity to play professional baseball. The Racine Belles, Kenosha Comets, South Bend Blue Sox and the Rockford Peaches played in the league's inaugural season in 1943. The teams were mostly based in the Midwest states of Illinois, Indiana, and Wisconsin.

The AAGPBL featured intense competition, with teams displaying great athleticism, speed, and ability on the field. The participants were talented and motivated athletes who worked hard to compete in the newly formed league.

During the inaugural season, one of the most notable plays in AAGPBL history occurred. Lavonne "Pepper" Paire Davis of the Rockford Peaches made an outstanding defensive play on May 30, 1943, in the league's first night game. Janet Rumsey of the Racine Belles hit a line drive along the third baseline with two outs in the bottom of the ninth inning and the score knotted. Paire Davis dove and snagged the ball in mid-air, securing the out and keeping the Peaches in the game. This play was dubbed the "million-dollar stop" and is still regarded as one of the most outstanding in AAGPBL history.

As the league grew, it broadened its scope, adding more clubs and players from various regions. The Minneapolis Millerettes and the Fort Wayne Daisies were added to the league in 1948, significantly expanding its representation.

The "closer rule," which permitted pitchers to enter games in relief, was established by the AAGPBL in 1948. This rule gave a new strategic component to the game and assigned specific roles to pitchers, similar to modern-day baseball.

Lavonne "Pepper" Paire Davis, who made that memorable play in 1943, became the first woman to play professional baseball in Japan in 1947, which was one of the most significant events in AAGPBL history. Her journey with the All-Star team helped to promote women's baseball internationally and brought the league a lot of attention.

Despite its triumphs, the AAGPBL experienced hurdles in the early 1950s, including financial difficulties and dwindling enrollment. The Kalamazoo Lassies, the Grand Rapids Chicks, the South Bend Blue Sox, the Fort Wayne Daisies, and the Rockford Peaches were the league's final five clubs in 1954.

The AAGPBL discontinued operations following the 1954 season. However, the memory of the league and the performances of its players have left an indelible mark on the world of sports. In recent years, AAGPBL players have been recognized for their achievements, and the league's history has been commemorated in museums, movies, and exhibitions.

The AAGPBL's trailblazing efforts and extraordinary skill have inspired generations of female athletes and acted as a tribute to the power of persistence, enthusiasm, and breaking down barriers in chasing aspirations, both on and off the baseball diamond.

The triumphs and trials of baseball's most legendary teams have woven a rich tapestry that continues to captivate fans, teaching us that baseball is more than just a game; it is a source of inspiration, community, and never-ending excitement.

Chapter 7
Little League Starter Guide for Beginners

Welcome to the exciting world of baseball! Whether you're stepping up to the plate for the first time or want to be a better player, this chapter will help you understand the fundamentals of playing little league in a simple way.

1. Hitting

Hitting a baseball can be challenging, but with the right technique, practice, and mindset, you'll be well on your way to becoming a successful batter.

Stance and Grip

The foundation of a good swing starts with your stance. Position yourself in the batter's box with your feet shoulder-width apart and knees slightly bent.

Maintain a loose grip on the baseball bat. Grab the handle of the bat with your fingers, just like you would with your bottom hand. Your index finger and bottom three fingers should be apart, but all four fingers should be holding the handle with your thumb in a comfortable place.

When holding a baseball bat, your dominant hand should be on top. Put the head of the bat in front of your lead foot on the ground. Take hold of the handle with your non-dominant or bottom hand. If you're a right-handed batter, your bottom hand and lead foot will be on the left side.

Proper Bat Swing

A successful swing involves a combination of coordination, timing, and balance. The mechanics of the swing can be broken down into several steps:

- **Load:** As the pitcher winds up, shift your weight back slightly and coil your body to generate power. As the pitcher releases the ball, take a small step forward with your front foot, pointing it toward the pitcher.

- **Transition:** Keep your weight balanced on the balls of your feet.
- **Swing:** As the ball approaches the strike zone, initiate your swing by turning your hips and shoulders, uncoiling the energy built up during the load phase. Keep your eyes on the ball and track it until contact.
- **Impact:** After making contact, extend your arms fully and follow through with your swing, allowing the bat to finish over your shoulder.

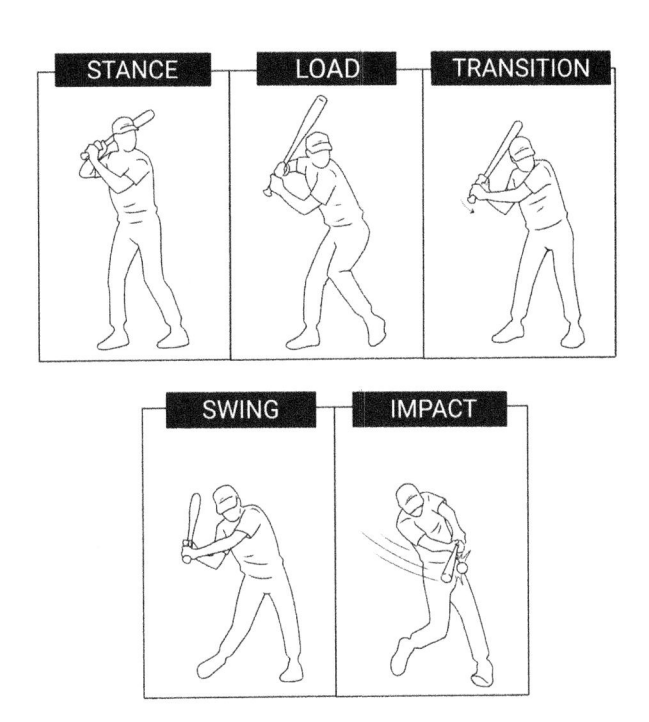

Understanding the Strike Zone

The strike zone is the area over home plate between the batter's knees and armpits. It's essential to recognize this zone and be selective about the pitches you swing at. Practice identifying the strike zone during batting practice, and work on developing a good eye for different styles of pitches.

Timing and Patience

Hitting a baseball requires excellent timing. Stay relaxed and be patient at the plate, waiting for the right pitch to swing at. Don't be afraid to take strikes early in the count to gather information about the pitcher's style and speed.

Mental Approach

Developing a strong mindset is just as important as having physical skills. Stay confident and positive at the plate, even if you have a few rough at-bats. Focus on the process rather than the outcome, and visualize successful swings before stepping into the batter's box.

Becoming a successful batter in little league baseball requires dedication, practice, and a positive mindset. Remember to work on your stance, grip, and swing mechanics, as well as understanding the strike zone and recognizing different pitches.

With time and effort, you'll see improvements in your hitting and enjoy the thrill of connecting with the ball, contributing to your team's success on the field.

2. Pitching

Pitching is a critical aspect of the game, and with the right techniques and mindset, you can become a successful pitcher and contribute significantly to your team's success.

Note: All directions are for a right-handed pitcher. If you are a lefty, follow the same steps, but do the opposite by mirroring each action.

Basic Pitching Mechanics

The foundation of successful pitching lies in mastering the basic mechanics. Proper pitching mechanics involve a series of coordinated movements to generate power, accuracy, and consistency.

Start with your feet shoulder-width apart on the pitching rubber, facing the catcher. Hold the ball in your glove hand and your pitching hand behind your back.

As you begin your wind-up, lift your front leg and stride forward with your lead foot, landing with it pointed toward home plate.

As your front foot lands, your throwing arm should come over the top in a circular motion, releasing the ball at the right time to achieve your desired pitch.

Grip and Pitches

Mastering different pitch grips is essential for becoming an effective pitcher. Here are some common pitches and their grips:

- **Fastball (2 & 4 Seam):** Hold the ball with your index and middle fingers placed together across the seams. Your thumb should rest under the ball for support. The fastball is your primary pitch, and you can throw it with four-seam or two-seam variations.
- **Slider:** Place your index and middle fingers across the seams of the baseball. Your forefinger should support the ball by resting underneath it. Hold it slightly asymmetrically, with your fingers on one side and your thumb on the other. This grasp formation will help you generate the spin necessary to cause the ball to move laterally when thrown.
- **Curveball:** Grip the ball with your index and middle fingers placed on the inside seam. Your middle finger should be slightly bent, creating topspin when you release the ball.
- **Changeup:** Hold the ball with three fingers (index, middle, and ring) on top of the ball and the thumb on the bottom. The changeup is meant to look like a fastball but with reduced speed to throw off the batter's timing.

4 Seam   2 Seam

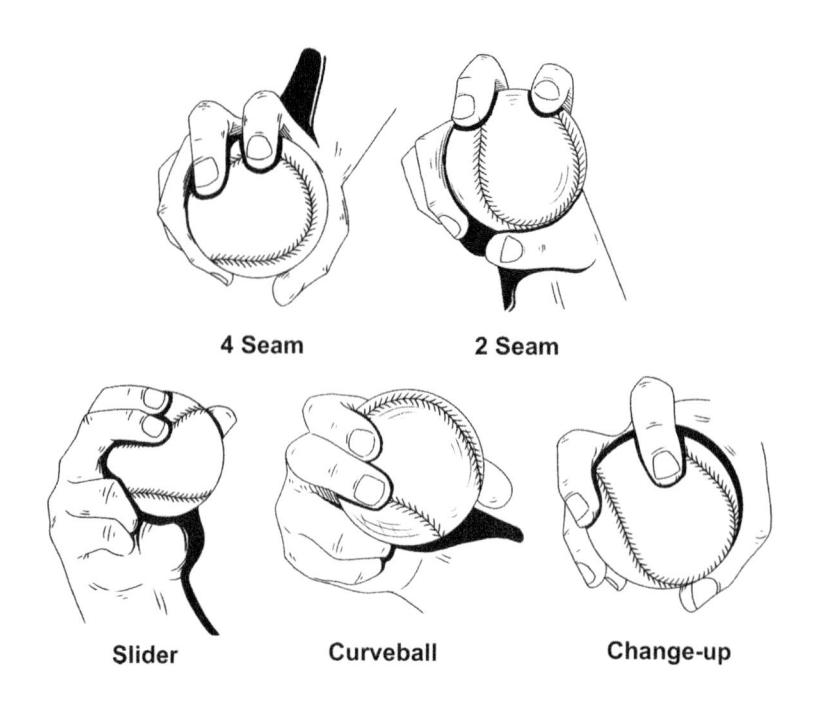

Slider   Curveball   Change-up

Developing Control and Accuracy

One of the most critical aspects of pitching is control and accuracy. It's essential to throw strikes consistently to keep the batter off balance and give your defense a chance to make plays.

Focus on maintaining a smooth and repeatable delivery. Consistency in your mechanics will lead to better control over your pitches.

Work on hitting your spots during practice. Aim for specific locations in the strike zone to improve your command.

Understanding the Strike Zone

The strike zone is the area over home plate between the batter's knees and armpits. It's essential to recognize the strike zone to know where to place your pitches effectively.

Practice pitching to a target or a catcher's glove placed in different areas of the strike zone to develop your ability to hit your spots consistently.

As a pitcher, you need to think strategically to keep batters guessing and off-balance. Plan your pitch sequences based on the batter's weaknesses and your strengths as a pitcher. Mix up your pitches to prevent hitters from sitting on a specific pitch.

Set up hitters by changing the speed and location of your pitches. For example, follow up a well-located fastball with a well-executed changeup.

Mental Approach

Pitching requires mental toughness and composure. Here are some tips for maintaining a strong mental approach:

- Stay focused on the next pitch. Don't dwell on past mistakes or successes; instead, concentrate on executing the next pitch.
- Trust your stuff. Believe in your abilities and your preparation, knowing that you have put in the work to succeed on the mound.

- Stay composed under pressure. Baseball is a game of ups and downs, and pitchers must remain level-headed during challenging situations.

Caring for Your Arm

As a young pitcher, it's essential to take care of your arm to prevent injuries and ensure long-term success. Follow a proper warm-up routine before pitching to prepare your arm for the stresses of throwing. It's important to avoid overuse and pitch counts.

Incorporate rest and recovery give your arm time to heal.

Becoming a successful pitcher in baseball involves mastering the basic mechanics, developing different pitches, and honing your control and accuracy. Understanding the strike zone and implementing effective pitch sequencing will keep batters off balance and improve your performance on the mound. Regular practice, mental toughness, and proper arm care are crucial elements in your journey to becoming a reliable and effective pitcher.

3. Fielding

Fielding is a crucial aspect of the game, and with the right techniques, practice, and mindset, you can become a skilled and confident fielder and contribute to your team's success.

Proper Fielding Stance

The foundation of successful fielding starts with adopting the proper fielding stance. Your stance should provide stability, agility, and readiness to react to the ball.

1. Stand with your feet shoulder-width apart and knees slightly bent, maintaining a balanced and athletic position.
2. Keep your glove hand out in front of you, with the glove open and fingers pointing upward, ready to receive the ball.
3. Position your body so that you are facing the batter or the direction of the play, staying alert and ready for action.

Fielding Ground Balls

Fielding ground balls is a fundamental skill for any baseball player.

- As the ball approaches, get your body down to the ground in a controlled manner, using small steps to adjust your position if needed.
- Position your glove directly in front of you and use your other hand to create a "triangle" with your glove, forming a target for the ball.
- Keep your eyes on the ball as it comes toward you and watch it into your glove, making sure to secure it with two hands once it's in your glove.
- Once you have fielded the ball, transfer it quickly from your glove to your throwing hand to prepare for the throw.

Fielding Fly Balls

Fielding fly balls can be both exhilarating and challenging. Here's how to field them effectively:

- Position yourself under the ball by reading its trajectory and adjusting your position accordingly.
- As the ball descends, track it with your eyes and use your glove hand to make any necessary adjustments.
- Catch the ball at the highest point possible, with your glove hand extended fully and your throwing hand securing the ball.

After making the catch, be prepared to make a quick and accurate throw if there are baserunners trying to advance.

Throwing Mechanics

Strong and accurate throws are crucial for successful fielding. Work on your throwing mechanics to improve your accuracy and arm strength.

- Start with your feet shoulder-width apart, facing your target.
- As you prepare to throw, step forward with your front foot, transferring your weight onto your back foot.
- As you release the ball, point your front shoulder toward your target, follow through with your arm, and use your whole body to generate power.

Position-Specific Fielding

Different positions on the field require specific fielding techniques and responsibilities. Here's a brief overview of key positions:

- Infielders: Infielders play closer to the batter and are responsible for fielding ground balls and making quick, accurate throws to get outs.
- Outfielders: Outfielders cover more ground in the outfield and are primarily responsible for catching fly balls and preventing extra-base hits.
- Catcher: The catcher is the backbone of the defense, receiving pitches from the pitcher and making throws to catch baserunners stealing.
- First Baseman: The first baseman's primary role is to field throws from other fielders and make plays at first base.

Communication and Teamwork

Effective fielding requires good communication and teamwork with your fellow players. If you are in a better position to field the ball, call out "I got it" to let your teammates know. Always be ready to back up your teammates on any plays to prevent extra bases or errors.

Mental Approach

Fielding requires mental focus and a positive mindset. Pay attention to each pitch and be ready to react to any play that comes your way. Believe in your abilities and trust your training. Confidence will help you make plays more effectively.

Becoming a skilled fielder in little league baseball requires mastering proper fielding techniques, including ground balls and fly balls, developing strong throwing mechanics, and understanding position-specific responsibilities. Regular practice, effective communication, and teamwork are essential elements of successful fielding.

4. Baserunning & Stealing

Base running is a crucial aspect of the game, and understanding the fundamentals of base running and stealing can give your team a competitive edge.

Base Running Fundamentals

Base running involves more than just running fast. It requires a combination of speed, technique, and smart decision-making. Here are some base running fundamentals to keep in mind:

- Start with a good lead: When on base, take a few steps away from the base in the direction of the next base to get a head start.
- Stay alert: Pay attention to the pitcher and the ball's location, as you might need to react quickly to take an extra base or return to the base safely.

- Round the bases smoothly: When advancing from one base to another, take a wide turn around the base to maintain momentum and shorten the distance to the next base.

Base Running Rules

Understanding the rules of base running is essential to avoid making costly mistakes on the field. Here are some key rules to keep in mind:

- You must touch each base in the correct order to score a run.
- If the defense tags you with the ball or the ball beats you to the base, you are out.
- When the ball is in play, you must stay within the baseline to avoid interference with fielders.

Stealing Basics

Stealing bases will give your team a significant advantage. Here are some easy to remember steps:

- Timing is critical: Pay attention to the pitcher's delivery to the plate. Time your jump off the base when the pitcher is about to release the ball.
- Quick first step: Explosive speed off the base is essential to beat the throw from the catcher.

- Read the catcher: Watch the catcher's movements to predict when they will throw to the base. If you anticipate a throw, slide or dive to avoid the tag.

Base Running Strategies

Successful base running involves more than just running fast. It requires strategic thinking and situational awareness. Here are some strategies to consider:

- Tagging up: When a fly ball is hit to the outfield, wait for the ball to be caught before attempting to advance to the next base. If the outfielder's throw is weak or offline, you can take advantage of their mistake and advance.
- Taking the extra base: If the defense is slow to react or makes a mistake, look for opportunities to take an extra base. For example, if the outfielder bobbles the ball, consider advancing to the next base.
- Hit and run: On a hit and run play, the base runner takes off from the base when the batter makes contact with the ball. This strategy can create gaps in the defense and help the batter advance safely.

Sliding Techniques

Sliding and diving are essential skills for base runners, especially when trying to avoid a tag or reach a base safely.

Bent leg slide: This slide involves approaching the base with one knee bent and the other leg extended behind you. As you slide, reach out with the hand closest to the base while keeping the other hand away from the fielder. Lean slightly towards the base and angle your body away from the fielder, maintaining a low position to reduce the risk of being tagged. This technique aims to create a smaller target and avoid collisions while sliding into the base.

Diving: A "forward dive" is a diving motion used by baserunners to avoid being tagged out when reaching a base. It entails leaning forward and downward while slipping headfirst into the base. To execute a proper baseball forward dive, begin the dive a short distance before the base, leading with your hands and head. As you slide headfirst, extend your arms forward and tuck your body, hoping to touch the base with your hand. Maintain a low body position and avoid making contact with fielders while prioritizing safety and quickness.

Mental Approach

Base running and stealing require mental sharpness and quick decision-making. Anticipate the play. Pay attention to the game situation and anticipate what might happen next. Be prepared to react to different scenarios on the field. Remember to stay aggressive. Base running often involves taking risks to gain an advantage for your team. Be confident and aggressive in your base running decisions.

As you take your first steps into the thrilling world of Little League, keep in mind that each swing, catch, and throw is a chance to improve your skills and become a better player. Always do your best, help out your teammates, and keep learning; these are the cornerstones of success that we've discussed so far. Know that every play is important, every progress is a win, and every moment spent with teammates on the field is valuable. Keep at it, play with all your heart, and never forget that any success is something to be celebrated!

Chapter 8
Baseball Trivia for Young Fans

In this final chapter, prepare to be surprised by the feats, facts, and grandeur that have made baseball a vital part of our cultural legacy.

Whether you're new to baseball history or a seasoned fan eager to add more stunning information to your arsenal, prepare to be astonished, amazed, and left in wonder by the incredible trivia that baseball has to offer. So put on your thinking cap, prepare to be enlightened, and join us as we explore the fascinating world of baseball trivia!

Teams

- From 1918 until 2004, the Boston Red Sox experienced an 86-year championship drought, which was commonly linked to the trade of Babe Ruth to the New York Yankees in 1919. This deal resulted in the "Curse of the Bambino," which was broken in 2004 when the Red Sox won the World Series.

- From 1908 to 2016, the Chicago Cubs had a 108-year championship drought. The "Curse of the Billy Goat" was attributed to the Chicago Cubs' refusal to allow a goat named Murphy into Wrigley Field during the 1945 World Series. When the Cubs won the World Series in 2016, the curse was finally broken.

- In 1903, the Pittsburgh Pirates defeated the Boston Americans (now the Red Sox) in a best-of-nine series.

- As of 2021, the New York Yankees hold the record for the most World Series championships, with 27.

- The Los Angeles Dodgers began as the Brooklyn Dodgers before relocating to Los Angeles in 1958. They were also known as the Los Angeles Angels until changing their name to the Dodgers.

. . .

- The St. Louis Cardinals have long-standing rivalries with both the Chicago Cubs (going back to 1892) and the Cincinnati Reds, making the National League Central one of the most competitive divisions in baseball.

- The San Francisco Giants' rivalry with the Los Angeles Dodgers dates back to when both teams played in New York as the New York Giants and Brooklyn as the Brooklyn Dodgers.

- The Atlanta Braves, who originally played in Boston, relocated to Milwaukee and changed their name there before settling in their current home in Atlanta. It wasn't until 1966 that they called Atlanta home.

- On April 6, 1977, the California Angels (now the Los Angeles Angels) faced the Seattle Mariners in the franchise's inaugural regular season game. It was a 7-0 victory for the Mariners.

- When the Houston Astros moved from the National League to the American League in 2013, they also moved to a new division. They did this without relocating, making them the first MLB franchise to do it.

- The Atlanta Braves, founded as the Boston Red Stockings in 1871, are the oldest continuously operating professional baseball franchise.

- As of 2023, the New York Yankees have won the most World Series championships with 27 victories.

- Longest Championship Drought: The 2016 World Series victory by the Chicago Cubs terminated their 108-year championship drought. Their prior title dated back to 1908.

- With 26 consecutive victories, the 1916 New York Giants retain the record for the longest winning streak in MLB history. This benchmark remains intact.

- In Game 5 of the 1920 World Series, Bill Wambsganss of the Cleveland Indians completed the only unassisted triple play in World Series history.

- Rickey Henderson holds the record for the most stolen bases in Major League Baseball history with 1,406 during his career.

- The quickest game in MLB history took place on September 28, 1919, between the New York Giants and Philadelphia Phillies. The contest only lasted 51 minutes.

- Don Larsen of the New York Yankees pitched the only perfect game in the annals of the World Series in Game 5 of the 1956 World Series against the Brooklyn Dodgers.

- The 1869 formation of the Cincinnati Red Stockings is regarded as the first professional baseball team. They were National Association of Professional Base Ball Players members.

- Most Legends of the Game on a Team: Five future Hall of Famers were on the roster of the 1936 New York Yankees: Babe Ruth, Lou Gehrig, Joe DiMaggio, Bill Dickey, and Lefty Gomez.

Ballparks and Stadiums

• The "Green Monster," a 37-foot-tall left-field wall, is a recognizable element of the Boston Red Sox's historic ballpark, Fenway Park. It is one of the most distinctive and iconic parts of any ballpark.

• Wrigley Field, the longtime ballpark of the Chicago Cubs, is famous for its ivy-covered outfield walls. The ivy makes the ballpark more attractive and unique.

• Spectacular views of downtown Pittsburgh and the Allegheny River can be seen from PNC Park, the home of the Pittsburgh Pirates. It is often considered to be among the most beautiful of all Major League Baseball stadiums.

• Located in Yankee Stadium, Monument Park, pays tribute to the New York Yankee's legendary players and landmark moments.

• McCovey Cove is an area of San Francisco Bay beyond the right-field wall where fans in kayaks and boats wait to grab home run balls at AT&T Park (now Oracle Park), home of the San Francisco Giants.

- The historic home of the Los Angeles Dodgers, Dodger Stadium, features palm trees behind the outfield line to provide a uniquely Californian atmosphere.

- A beautiful water extravaganza at center field at Kauffman Stadium, home of the Kansas City Royals, known as the "Water Spectacular Fountain," features a display of water and lights after every Royals home run and victory.

- A magnificent and meaningful icon, the statue of a snarling tiger stands near the main entrance to Comerica Park, the ballpark where the Detroit Tigers play.

- The Baltimore Orioles' home field, Oriole Park at Camden Yards, is famous for its vintage style. This design inspired a wave of other ballparks to be constructed with a similar, throwback aesthetic.

- The replica 19th-century train at Houston Astros' home ballpark Minute Maid Park follows a track above the left-field fence. The train starts to move and make whistle noises whenever the Astros hit a home run.

- Every time the Philadelphia Phillies score a home run, the 19-foot-tall replica of the Liberty Bell in center field rings.

- The heating system beneath the playing field at Target Field, home of the Minnesota Twins, is state-of-the-art. Thanks to this ingenious mechanism, the field may be used even when temperatures drop.

- The Rogers Centre, home of the Toronto Blue Jays, has a retractable roof that may be opened or closed depending on the weather. It was MLB's first ballpark with a fully working retractable roof.

- Miller Park, home of the Milwaukee Brewers, features a retractable fan-shaped roof. When closed, the roof mimics a fan, and when opened, it gives fans with an open-air experience.

MLB History

- In the 1860s, the phrase "major league" was first used to distinguish the top professional teams from amateur clubs. When the National League was created in 1876, it was legally adopted.

- The Cincinnati Red Stockings were the first openly professional baseball team, having been created in 1869. They were the first professional team to go undefeated in their first season.

- Before the era of segregation in baseball, African-American players such as Moses Fleetwood Walker and his brother Welday Walker played in the major leagues in the late 1800s.

- The first official World Series was played between the National League champion Pittsburgh Pirates and the American League champion Boston Americans (now the Red Sox) in 1903. The Americans won the best-of-nine series by a score of 5-3.

- When the New York Yankees first joined the American League in 1901, they were known as the Baltimore Orioles. They were known as the New York Highlanders after moving to New York in 1903, before adopting the Yankees name in 1913.

- On April 15, 1947, Jackie Robinson joined the Brooklyn Dodgers, shattering baseball's racial barrier and making him the first African-American player in the modern era.

- The first night game in Major League Baseball history was played on May 24, 1935, at Cincinnati's Crosley Field between the Reds and the Philadelphia Phillies.

- In 1929, the Cleveland Indians became the first MLB team to wear uniform numbers on their jerseys. The attempt, however, was short-lived and was not revived until the late 1930s.

- Lip Pike, a skilled baseball player in the mid-1800s, is regarded as the first professional player since he publicly accepted money for his services, breaking the amateur norm.

Player's Records and Statistics

- With 7,356 innings pitched, Cy Young retains the record for the most innings pitched in a career. This remarkable accomplishment was accomplished predominantly with the Cleveland Spiders and the Boston Red Sox.

- Cy Young also retains the record for the most wins by a pitcher in his career, with 511 victories. He played for the Cleveland Spiders, the Boston Red Sox, the Cleveland Naps, and the Boston Rustlers during his legendary career.

- Most Complete Games in a Season: In 1901, while playing for the St. Louis Cardinals, Jack Taylor set the record for most complete games in a season with an astounding 187.

- From 1986 to 2012, Jamie Moyer's unbroken career spanned an extraordinary 25 seasons, making it the longest career without interruption. He played for numerous organizations, including the Chicago Cubs, the Texas Rangers, the Seattle Mariners, and the Philadelphia Phillies.

- The 1950 Boston Red Sox turned a record 217 double plays in a single season, setting a new record. This remarkable accomplishment contributed to their success that year.

. . .

- In 1988, Orel Hershiser pitched 59 consecutive innings without allowing a run to establish the record for the most consecutive scoreless innings pitched. This feat was accomplished while playing for the Los Angeles Dodgers.

- Ichiro Suzuki of the Seattle Mariners set the record for the most hits in a single season in 2004 with 262 hits. This extraordinary achievement solidified his status as a hitting phenomenon.

- Most victories in a Single Season by a Team: With 116 victories each, the 1906 Chicago Cubs and 2001 Seattle Mariners share the record for most wins in a single season by a team. Frank Chance managed the Cubs to a record-setting season, while Lou Piniella led the Mariners to an outstanding season.

- Chief Wilson, who played for the Pittsburgh Pirates in 1912, set the record for the most triples in a single season with 36. This record for the most triples scored in a single season still stands.

- While playing for the Boston Red Sox, Manny Ramirez donated his dreadlocks to a foundation that creates wigs for children with cancer.

- Yogi Berra, the New York Yankees' Hall of Fame catcher, was noted for his amusing and often baffling "Yogi-isms," such as "It ain't over till it's over" and "When you come to a fork in the road, take it."

- Jim Abbott, who was born without a right hand, threw a no-hitter for the New York Yankees against the Cleveland Indians on September 4, 1993, demonstrating his exceptional pitching ability.

- Randy Johnson, noted for his scorching fastball, accidentally hit a bird with a pitch during a spring training game in 2001. The episode went down in baseball history as a legendary and odd moment.

- Johnny Vander Meer is the first player in MLB history to throw consecutive no-hitters. He accomplished this astounding achievement while playing for the Cincinnati Reds in 1938.

- Bob Feller, a great Cleveland Indians pitcher, is the only pitcher to have struck out 12 or more batters in four different no-hitters.

- Billy Sunday, a skilled outfielder in the early twentieth century, went on to become a well-known preacher who led religious revivals across the United States.

- Sadaharu Oh, a Japanese baseball player, holds the world record for the most career home runs with 868, which he accomplished while playing for the Yomiuri Giants.

- In 2001, Barry Bonds set the single-season home run record with 73 home runs for the San Francisco Giants, beating Mark McGwire's previous record.

- Pete Rose has 4,256 career hits, which is the most in MLB history. Despite his achievements, he is ineligible for the Hall of Fame because of his suspension from baseball for gambling.

- Mariano Rivera, the renowned New York Yankees closer, has the most career saves in MLB history with 652, making him one of the most dominant relief pitchers in history.

. . .

- Rickey Henderson holds the all-time stolen base record with 1,406 steals, which is unlikely to be broken in the current era of baseball.

- Known as the "Iron Horse," Lou Gehrig played in 2,130 consecutive games before being diagnosed with amyotrophic lateral sclerosis (ALS).

- Mickey Mantle was recognized for his enormous power, and he was one of the few players to hit tape-measure home runs, some of which traveled more than 600 feet.

- Honus Wagner's baseball card is one of the world's most valuable and desired memorabilia. Collectors treasure the uncommon T206 Wagner card.

- Reggie Jackson gained the nickname "Mr. October" after his spectacular performance for the New York Yankees in the 1977 World Series, when he hit three home runs in a single game.

- Cy Young is the only pitcher in Major League Baseball history to have won 500 games. He pitched for 22 seasons and won his final game at the age of 44, demonstrating his endurance and talent.

- For 33 years, Hank Aaron held the all-time home run record, hitting 755 home runs over his long career. Barry Bonds eventually exceeded his record. In addition to his 755 home runs, Hank Aaron had 3,771 hits during his storied career, making him one of baseball's most accomplished hitters.

- Pitcher Nolan Ryan owns the MLB record for the most career strikeouts with 5,714, demonstrating his endurance and dominance on the mound.

- On Sept 6. 1995, Cal Ripken Jr. broke Lou Gehrig's long-standing record by playing in 2,632 consecutive games.

The rich tapestry of MLB baseball trivia not only reveals the astounding accomplishments of individual players and teams, but also provides a unique lens through which to view the growth of the sport. Each record contains stories of perseverance, skill, teamwork, and the constantly evolving strategies that define baseball. These records enhance not only your baseball trivia knowledge, but also your appreciation for the subtleties of the game-- connecting its past to the present and providing insight into its future.

Conclusion

Baseball, with its rich history and memorable events, continues to inspire new generations of fans and players. The spirit of the game has remained intact from the early days of sandlots and makeshift fields to the grandeur of modern stadiums, a monument to its enduring appeal. Throughout this book, we've unearthed the fascinating stories of renowned players who engraved their names in the books of baseball history, as well as the unforgettable games that continue to ring in the ears of baseball fans around the world.

Aspiring young players on the diamond might draw inspiration from their baseball heroes' drive and desire. Baseball is about more than hitting home runs or throwing scorching fastballs; it's about collaboration, sportsmanship, and striving for excellence. Use the supplied tips and tactics to develop your skills and enjoy the game.

Let this guide serve as a reminder of the beauty and togetherness that define baseball when the crack of the bat and cheers from the stands fill the air.

Understanding the origins of the game, the legendary players who have adorned the field, and the evolving strategies over time equips you with a deeper understanding of the essence of the sport. As a young player or fan, this information not only fuels your passion for baseball, but also enables you to appreciate the sport's values of teamwork, tenacity, and sportsmanship. You stand at the crossroads of baseball's past and future, prepared to leave your imprint on the diamond and write your own chapter in the illustrious history of this beloved sport!

Printed in Great Britain
by Amazon